Contents

Preface

Normally, the preface of a cat-care book notifies the reader about all the worthwhile and invaluable information to be found in the ensuing pages. In addition, the author sternly admonishes the reader that owning a cat is a solemn responsibility. Before doing that, however, I will tell you briefly how a kitten is made.

The magical orchestration that delivers a kitten to your trust begins at conception, when sperm and egg fuse, nuclei merge, genes become paired, and a new organism is formed. By day 5 of its 63-day gestation period, this infinitesimal life, which already is able to absorb simple nutrients, emerges from the oviduct where it was conceived and enters one of the horns of the Y-shaped uterus. Five or six days later the hopeful snippet of existence, all of four millimeters long, docks gently against the uterine wall from whence the developing embryo will draw sustenance until its birth.

That embryo begins to change shape considerably between the eighteenth and twenty-fourth days of gestation, becoming elongated and displaying the early formation of a tail. At the other end of the embryo the division between head and trunk becomes pronounced, different sections of the brain are established, limbs begin to form, and the features unique to the family, genus, and species of the cat begin to develop. By then the fetus measures scarcely more than half an inch in length, yet the earliest recognizable forms of the liver, the respiratory system, the limbs, sense organs, skull, and urogenital structures are all in place.

The final segment of gestation, the fetal-growth period, begins about day 24 and lasts until birth. The organization and development of the various systems that take place in the fetal-growth period transform those systems from a prefunctional to a functional state—all in anticipation of the day when the fetus will begin an independent life outside the womb. It is astonishing that so much of such consequence is happening in so small a space. During the fetal-growth period—at the same time and in the same minute enclosure—a skeleton is developing that will support the cat; muscles that will transport the cat are strapping themselves securely to that skeleton; the circulatory system that will carry blood throughout the cat's body is laying down the roadways to support that journey; and an interdisciplinary network of systems is being perfected that will make the cat the proud, graceful, ineffable creation that it is.

This, in short, is how a kitten is made. If all the work that Nature does to provide you with a kitten does not inspire you to take good care of it, I do not know what will. If you are suitably inspired, however, there is a lot of worthwhile and invaluable information in this book that will help you to keep your end of the bargain.

Chapter 1 asks you to examine your motives for acquiring a kitten. Are you looking for companionship, a wrestling buddy for your present cat, a playmate for your children, a replacement for a former pet, or a gift for a friend? Or are you interested in breeding and showing? All motives are not created equal, and Chapter 1 will help you to sort through and evaluate yours.

Chapter 2, "Where to Find a Kitten," considers the places where you might find a kitten or a kitten might find you. Friends, relatives, neighbors, breeders, the cat next door, Mother Nature, humane societies, and pet stores all have kittens to offer. Where is the best place to acquire yours?

In Chapter 3 certain myths that have attached themselves like barnacles to purebred cats are debunked. There are roughly 50 breeds of cats, and only a fool or a writer on assignment would try to make anyone believe that each one of those breeds has its own separate and distinct personality. You will not be apt to believe it yourself after you have finished this chapter.

"Choosing the Right Kitten" (Chapter 4) will help you decide whether you want a male or a female, one kitten or two, a show cat or a pet. This chapter also provides tips on selecting a healthy kitten, assessing a kitten's personality, and making your way through the paperwork that often accompanies purchasing or adopting a kitten.

Chapter 5, "Living with a New Kitten," provides a list of materials you will need before you bring your new kitten home, presents hints on how to make your house kitten-proof, and describes the best way to introduce your kitten to its new surroundings.

Making sure your kitten is well fed is the domain of Chapter 6, which tells you how much and how often you should feed your kitten, what foods are acceptable, and what foods you should avoid. What's more, this chapter tells you how to decipher a cat food label.

Chapter 7, "Training a New Kitten," explains how kittens learn and why they misbehave. This chapter also presents strategies for teaching your kitten to respond to its name, developing good litter pan manners in your kitten, and teaching your pet to use its scratching post. In addition, Chapter 7 tells you how to discourage your kitten from begging and from chewing on things you do not want it to chew.

Chapter 8, "Kitten Care and Grooming," reveals how often you should groom your kitten, describes how you should go about doing it, and identifies the tools you will need to do the job properly.

"The Kitten's Body Works" (Chapter 9) is a reference chapter that describes in some detail the physiology of cats, inside and out. Sight, hearing, taste, smell, touch, muscles, skeleton, intelligence— information to which new kitten owners will want to return as they grow up with their kittens.

In Chapter 10, "The Healthy Kitten," you will learn how preventive medicine can keep your kitten healthy; you will be coached in recognizing symptoms that indicate illness; and you will be told how to care for a sick kitten.

Chapter 11, "Understanding and Communicating with Your Kitten," explores the feline psyche, which is not so mysterious as some would have you believe. Indeed, the more you know about the effects of evolution and domestication on your kitten's behavior, the less you will be confounded by your pet's habits and the better you will be able to communicate with your kitten.

Contracts, the subject of Chapter 12, are a fact of life for people who buy or adopt kittens. Once you understand the facts, you will not become snaggled in the fine print.

Whether you are thinking about acquiring a kitten or have just acquired one, I hope this book will make everyday life more enjoyable for you and your kitten for many years to come.

Phil Maggitti
Spring 1995

Chapter 1
Why Do You Want a Kitten?

I almost bought a kitten last weekend. I was not planning on buying a kitten when I left the house. Of course, many people who buy or find or adopt kittens were not planning on buying, finding, or adopting a kitten when they left the house either, but kittens have a way of sneaking up on a body.

The kitten I almost bought was a Himalayan, a longhair with Siamese markings and a Persian face and body. The kitten and three of its litter-mates were sitting in a cage in the picture-framing shop where I had gone to pick up a Wyeth print (every house in southeastern Pennsylvania has to have at least one Wyeth print) and the official American Kennel Club certificate of championship that had been won by one of our pug dogs.

I walked into the frame shop, minding my own business, and there were the kittens, cuter than all get out, eyes the palest blue, faces as *rasa* as any *tabula* could be. Before I could stop myself, I was thinking of how much fun it would be to have a kitten around again and of how surprised and happy my wife would be

when she arrived home later that day and found me watching football with a kitten on my lap. I even began rehearsing my speech: "What kitten? Oh, this one. I found her in the yard by the garage. She must have escaped from the cat show that was in town a few weeks ago." Finally, my resolve beginning to wither, I asked the frame shop guy how much the kittens cost. He informed me that the prices ranged from $175 to $250. Because the kittens did not look very old, I inquired after their ages.

"They're seven weeks old," the framer replied.

The price was certainly good. The kittens' age was not. Perhaps that was why I decided I was not going to buy one. If people have any say about it, kittens should be at least 12 weeks old before they leave their mothers. I had just made that point in this very manuscript, so I did not think I should be an accomplice in the sale of an under-age kitten. Besides, we have eight cats already, and if we add to that number, soon we are going to reach the point of diminishing

1

This kitten's ears are in the can't-believe-my-ears position.

attention, and the cats' quality of life is going to suffer. Therefore, the side of my brain that is supposed to be responsible said to the side of my brain that lives for temptation, "Thou shalt not buy that kitten."

While I am parading my virtue, common sense, and restraint, I should mention that I have not always been able to resist the impulse to buy, find, or adopt a kitten. I would not have eight cats otherwise, but cute is not among the best reasons for buying a kitten—or adopting one for that matter—and if you are considering buying, finding, or adopting a kitten, I hope you stop for a second before you do and ask yourself why you want that kitten.

The motivation for acquiring a kitten is far more important than the means by which a kitten is acquired—unless the kitten you acquire is already owned by someone else. What's more, acquiring a kitten is not a political assertion, a fashion statement, or a declaration of moral superiority. It is a personal decision for which you need not have to answer to anyone but yourself and those with whom you live.

Companionship

We all know that cats are good for us. They seldom interrupt when we are talking. They are always ready to assist at nap time. They are wonderful at keeping secrets, at keeping themselves clean, and at keeping loneliness at bay. They have even been credited with lowering our blood pressure.

The best reason for getting a kitten is to enjoy the pleasure of its company. If you never have experienced the joy of watching a kitten come to terms with the world—and trying to bend the world to its terms—your life is poorer for want of that experience. Kittens are all eyes, ears, and innocence. They are ineffably soft, unerringly cute, unfailingly mischievous, and surprisingly resilient. They can make you laugh when you have no reason to, and they can drag a smile from your soul on the most tight-lipped day. Such is their influence that it is almost impossible not to grin at anyone you meet who is wearing a T-shirt with a kitten on it, just as one is always happy to hear from anyone who sends a greeting card with a kitten on the cover.

In order to deserve companionship, however, you must be willing to provide it. If you do not enrich your kitten's life as much as it enriches yours, you are taking advantage of your kitten's good nature. Your kitten will always be ready to lick your face when the heel marks of a frustrating day are stamped across your brow. When you are keyed up because of something the boss, the clerk at the convenience store, the person in the next cubicle at work, the president, some editorial writer, a loved one, the neighbor's kid, or all of the above did or said recently, your kitten will be happy to sit and listen to you discourse about the unfairness of it all. If you are a good kitten owner, you will be ready to return the favor.

A Chum for Your Other Cat

Kittens are also adept at cheering up members of their own species. If you are acquiring your first kitten, you should think seriously about acquiring two, even if there is always someone at home during the day and your kitten will not have to spend great amounts of time alone. In addition to human company, kittens should enjoy the company of their own kind.

If you have a cat already and that cat is still of flexible age, no more than five years old, it is not too late

to add a second cat to the household, providing you manage the introduction properly. (See Introducing Other Pets, page 40.)

Crashing through the defense, the gray kitten scores the game's winning touchdown.

For the Kid(s)

"We are given children to test us and to make us more spiritual," writes columnist George F. Will. Unfortunately, some parents give their children pets for similar reasons; but pets are not teaching devices, and spirituality may be beyond the reach of most adults, let alone children. Parents, therefore, should never buy a pet for their children "only if you promise that you're going to take care of it. Or else I'll take it back." Children will make that promise readily, but if a child reneges and Mom or Dad winds up taking care of the pet, the child has learned the rewards of irresponsibility. Or if, heaven forbid, the parent

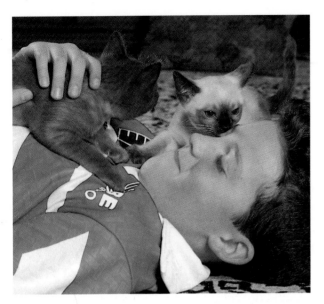

Kids make the best kitten beds.

Because they do not always understand that what is fun for them may be painful for a kitten, children must be taught to be careful walking and playing when the kitten is around. They must learn to speak and play quietly because kittens often are frightened by loud, unfamiliar sounds. They must be taught to pick up a kitten with one hand under the kitten's rib cage just behind the front legs and the other hand under the kitten's bottom. They must also receive the benefit of good example: if parents discipline a kitten by striking it, their children will, too.

Kittens can inspire a sense of responsibility in children, but children never should be forced to take care of kittens; and even when a child is a cooperative caretaker, parents should keep an unobtrusive eye on the kitten's feeding schedule, litter pan, and general condition. Parents should remember also that when they buy kittens for their youngsters, they are buying the kittens for themselves. Inevitably, even the most kitten-responsible youngsters grow up and leave home; and they do not always take their cats with them, especially when they go off to college.

makes good on the threat to get rid of the pet, the child learns that pets are disposable commodities—a lesson that is brought home all too often in this society.

Children cannot learn to take care of a kitten until they have learned to treat it properly. In fact, children who are too young or immature to appreciate a kitten can pose a threat to its safety and its sense of confidence. Children who live with kittens must be mature enough to understand that kittens do not like to be disturbed when they are eating or sleeping or using their litter pans, that there is a right way to hold a kitten, that kittens are not toys to be lugged around the house, and that a litter pan is not a sandbox. This is why parents with toddlers should wait until their children are roughly four years old before buying a kitten.

Caretakers are made, not born. Children do not come into the world equipped with a knowledge of how to take care of animals. This writer, for example, while still a preschooler, set out one day with a rag soaked in detergent to clean the spots off the neighbor's Dalmatian.

Understandably, when children are more ready than they are able to take care of the family cat, that is, when they are still preschoolers, their participation in cat care should be limited, structured, and closely supervised. If preschoolers want to help take care of a cat or kitten, they can hand their parents the cat's water bowl when it is time to wash and refill it each day; they can set the cat's food dish on the floor; watch as the cat is being groomed; or go along when Mom or Dad takes the cat to the veterinarian. These activities will provide a child with a sense of involvement with the cat's well-being.

After they are in school, children between the ages of five and seven should be capable of washing and refilling the water dish, under parental supervision at first, and of filling up the cat's dry food bowl. They also may be able to open cans of food and spoon the correct amount onto the cat's dish. Finally, children in the lower elementary grades should be capable of brushing or combing a cat gently. The ability to perform these tasks, however, should not be confused with the capacity to remember to do them each day. Parents will have to remind their children when it is time to feed or brush the cat— occasionally or more often, as the situation requires.

By the time a child is eight years old, he or she can be assigned more chores and greater responsibility, yet children in this age group still will require supervision. In addition to feeding the cat on their own, children in this age group can begin to scoop out the litter pan. They should be advised, though, of the necessity of washing their hands after cleaning the pan.

Teenagers, for all their fondness for loud music, cars, and clothing, can sometimes be counted on to take full responsibility for a cat's care. Parents should check nevertheless, without appearing to, of course, to see if a teenager's duties are being discharged faithfully.

Taking care of the family pet provides many people with their first taste of what it is like to be responsible for another living being. This responsibility can do wonders for a child's self-image and can help to instill a lifelong virtue of empathy. For its part, your cat will be grateful for the loving attention.

To Replace a Former Pet

Persons whose cats have died are often advised to go out and get another cat right away. For some people this is good advice; for others it is an insult. Only you can decide whether you need time to grieve over the loss of a cat or whether you need a new kitten to take your mind off your grief, but if you are looking for a kitten because your previous cat has died, do not expect the new kitten to be just like your old one. Your new kitten deserves to be loved for who he is, not resented for what he is not.

As a Gift for a Friend

"Hearts are not had as a gift but hearts are earned," wrote the Irish poet William Butler Yeats. The same applies to kittens. Quite simply, kittens are not for giving. It is presumptuous and risky to give someone a kitten, no matter what the occasion. The gesture might succeed occasionally, but more often than not this is an idea whose timing is unfortunate, and the kitten is frequently the one that suffers the consequences.

Breeding or Showing

Breeding a handsome, well-mannered kitten can provide joy, satisfaction, and the feeling of achievement that accompanies any creative endeavor. There is, however, a great responsibility attached to this undertaking. Too many pedigreed kittens are produced for the wrong reasons: ego gratification, monetary gain, or to provide the children an opportunity to witness the miracle of birth. At a time when 5 or 6 million cats are destroyed in animal shelters for lack of good homes each year, the decision to bring more kittens into the world is not one to be made lightly. For most people it is not one that should be made or even contemplated at all.

A gift kitten might seem like a great idea, but it could bring disappointment to all concerned.

Here are five good reasons why persons who consider bringing kittens into the world should weigh that decision carefully.

Before you buy a kitten for breeding, you should ask yourself why you want to do so. If your answers include winning fame and fortune in the cat world, perhaps you should consider a hobby that does not involve living creatures. Few breeders become overnight sensations; few litters are filled with nothing but show-quality kittens; and few people make money selling kittens. Indeed, making money is never a valid reason for breeding any animal.

If you are not certain you will make your kittens as happy as they make you—and that you can find homes for them that are as good as the one you will provide while they are in your care—then you should not set about making kittens at all. In fact, you never should produce a litter for which you do not have good homes already—or the unwa-vering intention of providing a good home, namely yours, for any kitten you cannot place. And do not include on your list of qualified, prospective owners any family member or friend who says casually that he or she would love to have a kitten. Those are not promises, they are wishes; and wishes generally evaporate a few minutes after you ring someone up and say, "I've got that kitten you were looking for."

If you are still with me at this point, perhaps you are merely curious, or perhaps you are the rare individual who is responsible enough to be entrusted with the privilege of raising kittens. If so, there are two more things you need to understand: much can go wrong in a planned mating, and in the animal world anything that can go wrong generally will, sooner or later.

Chapter 2
Where to Find a Kitten

During the 23 years I have owned cats, I have found them, or they have found me, in virtually every conceivable fashion. A friend or two has pressed a homeless cat on me. I have bought cats from breeders and in pet shops. I have found cats by the side of the road. Cats have found their way to the side, front, and back of my house, and I have adopted cats from animal shelters.

Cats have no bad sides. Either profile is a masterpiece.

Of the eight cats that we own at the present time, Bride and Skippy came from two different people we knew who just had to find homes for them; Chirp and Ginger, who is gray, figured they knew the house of a soft touch when they smelled one; Recky we bred ourselves; Rollo we found by the side of the road; and Jack and Syney were adopted from a shelter.

Each of these cats is unique, and each serves to illustrate the methods by which people acquire cats.

Friend, Relative, or Neighbor

In a survey conducted by Penn & Schoen Associates for The Humane Society of the United States in November 1992, nearly half the respondents (46 percent) said they had gotten their dogs or cats from a friend or relative. Unfortunately, the survey did not distinguish between sources of dogs and sources of cats, which it should have done. The survey did indicate, however, that dog owners were more than twice as likely to own pedigreed animals than were cat owners and that persons who adopted animals from shelters were "equally as [*sic*] likely to own a dog or cat or both." One can assume, therefore, that the combined figures for dog and cat owners approximate the figures for cat owners alone, as long as one keeps in mind that the combined percentages of dogs and cats acquired from breeders (18 percent) and from pet stores (9 percent) are probably overestimates of the percentages that would obtain for cats alone. Thus, friends and relatives with kittens in need are the sources from which most people acquire their kittens.

Friends of friends should be added to that category. We acquired two of our cats, Bride and Skippy, from friends of friends.

Bride came first, in the summer of 1985. We were at a demonstration cat show in a mall near Harrisburg, Pennsylvania. The demonstration show, sponsored by the cat club to which we belonged at the time, consisted of ten or so cats, sitting in cages in varying degrees of contentment. These cats represented some of the breeds that would be competing at the club's annual championship show, which was to be held in a few weeks.

While my wife was answering questions about our cats from noonday shoppers—and learning that every third shopper had "a cat just like that at home"—I was trying to hide inside a magazine. Eventually, a club member, a friend of a friend, came in toting a box and a

The director and the assistant directors on the set.

forlorn expression. Nowadays I would recognize that expression in an instant. Being less street smart then, I asked the friend of a friend what she had in the box.

What she had was four kittens and a tale of woe. The kittens, it seems, had been born under a trailer that belonged to an ailurophobe, who had threatened to drown the kittens come his first day off. This being Saturday and the ailurophobe's day off, it was sink-or-swim time for the kittens.

Luckily, a group of children had overheard the threats against the kittens, had rounded up a box, had stuffed the kittens into it, and had taken them to this friend of a friend's house because they knew she liked cats. The friend of a friend, in turn, had taken the kittens to the demonstration show, where she knew there would be a number of people who liked cats. With any luck and a little cajoling, she would return home with an empty box and a full heart.

I think I was the first one to rise to the bait—by this time my wife was trying to hide inside the magazine—selecting a brown mackerel tabby female from among the rescued kittens. We named the kitten Bride because we intended to use her when she grew up to prove a longhair Scottish fold male who was just beginning to feel his oats and, consequently, was looking to sow a few. The fact that Bride was not pedigreed and the kittens would not be registrable did not concern us. If this strikes the Sensitive Reader as callous and altogether too casual, remember that this was 1985; it was still morning in America, and pet overpopulation had yet to be elevated to the status of a national concern, even though millions of cats and kittens were put to sleep for lack of good homes that year.

Bride spent her first night in the kitchen of her new home. We had three other cats at the time, and the next day we began to let them get acquainted with their new housemate.

Bride had two kittens the following spring and was spayed four months later. She is our oldest cat and our most senior resident. Her kittens still live with the people to whom we gave them.

Skippy, who was acquired from friends of a friend, arrived at our house on Saturday January 26, 1991. We first had heard about Skippy from our friend AnnaBell, who lives in New York City but who was born and raised not far from where we live in southeastern Pennsylvania. AnnaBell is an inveterate cat rescuer, and she was trying to find a home for two young cats that were then residing at a veterinarian's office where they recently had undergone all manner of tests to insure that they were healthy.

AnnaBell, whose cat-rescuing range includes most of the North Atlantic states, was coming to Pennsylvania to assist in finding homes for the cats—Skippy and his sister, Risky. During the course of an especially memorable dinner at Joe's, an haute cuisine restaurant in Reading, Pennsylvania, I heard myself volunteering to let Skippy and Risky stay at my house until AnnaBell could find homes for them.

Needless to say, my offer to keep Skippy and his sister for a while eventually turned into an offer to keep them for good. Unfortunately, Risky died of lymphoma before we had had her for a month. Skippy, whom we had been keeping isolated with Risky, turned out to be fine and is one of our two indoor-outdoor cats today.

Breeders

Cat breeders—indeed, animal breeders of all stripes—do not enjoy the greatest of reputations these days. This is not to say that all kittens purchased from breeders are a cinch to die of some contagion within four to eight weeks, nor is it to say, as some animal rights advocates have claimed, that breeding animals is immoral. It is to say, however, that there are no intelligence or integrity tests required of persons who decide to take it upon themselves to breed and to sell cats. It is also to say that the person who advertises cats for sale may be a conscientious, compassionate individual motivated solely by the love of his or her chosen breed and the desire to contribute to its furtherance and perfection, or he or she might be a craven, opportunist who would sell a kitten to a band of devil worshipers as long as their checks did not bounce.

The point to remember when buying a kitten from a breeder is this: although temperament and good health are heritable to some degree, the way a kitten is raised is more important in shaping its personality and in determining its state of health. Kittens that are not handled often enough between the ages of three and fourteen weeks are less likely to develop into well-adjusted family members than are kittens that receive frequent handling and attention during this crucial time. Therefore, it is well to ask how many litters a breeder produces each year and how many other litters he or she was raising when the kitten you are interested in was growing up. A breeder who

produces more than three or four litters a year—or who was raising two or three other litters while your kitten's litter was maturing—may not have had time to socialize every kitten in those litters properly. A breeder who raises one or—at most—two litters at a time has more opportunity to give each of those kittens the individual attention it deserves. In general, the smaller the cattery, the more user-friendly the kittens it will produce and the more healthy those kittens will be.

A mother-and-children reunion, the kind that takes place several times a day while kittens are young.

Nature

On Halloween day 1992 my wife Mary Ann and I drove through a wooded section just south of Reading, Pennsylvania. Mary Ann noticed a tiny, bedraggled kitten trying to break into an empty chocolate milk carton by the side of the road. "Turn around," she said.

Cats can adapt to a wide range of environments, and one of their favorite ranges is the out-of-doors.

In the few minutes it took to turn around, the kitten had disappeared into the woods. Because we had our four pug dogs in the van, I bravely volunteered to wait by the side of the road while Mary Ann went looking for the kitten. While she was gone, I tried to remember the fastest route to the nearest hospital in case the kitten had rabies and an inclination to bite.

Five minutes later Mary Ann emerged from the woods with a sorry looking, malodorous mess of clumpy fur and bones masquerading as a kitten. Trouble was, it looked as if life had been all tricks and no treats for this little guy. We made him comfortable in the crate we keep in the van and managed to get to our vet's office only a few minutes after her noontime closing.

The vet took one look at the kitten, wrinkled her nose, and said "Yecch." On closer inspection she noted that the kitten, who we had guessed was about seven weeks old, had a full set of adult teeth with enough tartar on them to put his age at close to one year.

The tartar was the least of this dude's problems. He also had ear mites, frostbitten toes, an upper respiratory infection, five kinds of worms, and an abscess on his right flank that was too big and festering to suture. He was, in addition, dehydrated and severely malnourished. He weighed 2.5 pounds (1.1 kg). About the only thing he did not have was leukemia, so we took him home.

The vet was not sure the cat would last the weekend. She further explained that because he had a wound of unknown origin, he would have to be isolated from our other cats for five or six months in order to be sure he was not rabid. At that point, craven soul that I am, I was beginning to wish the cat had been a faster runner, but it is hard to motor on a festering, gimpy leg.

Mary Ann, however, was determined to save the cat. As we drove home, I remembered something her father had said to me the first time we met: "My daughter often sees good where none exists." I have wondered on more than one occasion if he was referring to me.

The cat, christened Rollo after the trailer park from which Bride had been rescued, survived the weekend, though for several days he urinated in his bed because he was too weak to drag himself the few feet to the litter pan in his cage.

After a couple of weeks, Mary Ann stopped wearing gloves when she handled Rollo. Shortly after that she gave him the run of an entire room; and finally, on a promising spring day in 1993, he had cleared quarantine and was allowed to work his way into the feline pecking order in our house, where he happily resides today.

If you are waiting for a moral to this story, it is this: In the current debate regarding the best ways to solve the pet overpopulation problem, the opponents of legislation that would effectively tax or regulate the activities of those who breed animals often argue that estimates of the number of unwanted animals killed in shelters each year are inflated and misleading. We are told that the number of cats killed in shelters—5.8 million for 1992 according to the American Humane Association—must be adjusted earthward because many of those cats, the majority some would argue, are unadoptable. They are unadoptable because they are too sick, too old, or too unruly to make good pets. Therefore, they should not be counted as part of the overpopulation problem.

This argument is naive and self-serving at best, cynical and self-serving at worst, and could not be farther from the truth. Rollo, the cat my wife was bent on saving, certainly would have been considered unadoptable, but Rollo, who now weighs 12 contented pounds (5.4 kg) and counting, is glad that some people see adoptability where others say it does not exist.

What's more, cats do not have to be at death's or an empty milk carton's door to be considered unadoptable. A cat may be "unadoptable" because it is suffering from a treatable illness that a shelter does not have the time, money, personnel, or volunteers to treat. One of those treatable illnesses is called kittenhood. If a shelter has too many kittens that are too young to be put up for adoption and too few people willing to provide foster homes until those kittens are old enough to be adopted, those "unadoptable" kittens will be euthanized. A cat also might be unadoptable because it is orange and the shelter has enough orange cats already in its adoption wing.

Whatever the reason cats are "unadoptable," make no mistake about it, each of those "unadoptable" cats was adoptable at some point in its life. They were not born "unadoptable," and if they are "unadoptable" now, it is because society has failed them. We will continue to fail them if we do not challenge the wisdom of anyone who persists in saying that "unadoptable" cats somehow do not count.

Humane Society

Anyone who can walk through the holding room at an animal shelter and not go home with a kitten

Sometimes kittens lie down to think. Other times they just lie down.

has either adopted a kitten recently, has so many cats already that he has to reserve a space in bed with a kitchen chair, or is heavily tranquilized. Because I answered to none of those descriptions when I visited the holding room at a local animal shelter shortly before Christmas 1993, there was no way I was not going to go home with a cat.

The cat's name is Jack. He is gray. He was about eight months old that Saturday when we saw one of his long, beckoning front legs reaching out of his cage. When I leaned toward his cage, he tapped me lightly on the nose, claws in, as if to say, "Hey, man, you're not going to find anything more friendly or amusing than me in this joint."

Jack was right. Matter of fact, I am not sure there is a cat any more friendly or amusing than Jack, period. Everyone from our cat sitter to a British cat writer and her hus-band who were visiting last Sunday is treated to the full Jack treatment, which includes wrapping his front legs around your neck and nuzzling you with his head, all the while purring louder than a food processor in overdrive.

Jack thoroughly refutes the arguments of the false prophets who declare that kittens and cats adopted from shelters are health or personality risks. On the contrary, kittens and cats put up for adoption are members of the all-star team of the feline world. Most shelters are so overstocked with kittens and cats that only the most healthy and sociable kittens are put up for adoption. The rest are euthanized.

Pet Store

Anyone who considers buying a pedigreed kitten from a pet shop should ask the pet shop owner for the name, address, and phone number of the kitten's breeder. If the pet shop owner is unwilling or unable to provide that information, the buyer should proceed with caution because he or she has less information about the kitten than normally would be available if the kitten was being purchased directly from its breeder.

If the pet shop owner provides the name and address of the kitten's breeder—and if that person lives nearby—the prospective customer would do well to visit the breeder to observe the conditions in which the kitten was raised. If the breeder lives far away, the prospective buyer should telephone to ask questions about the kitten that the pet shop operator might not be able to answer: How many other kittens were in the litter? How old was the kitten when it left its mother? How many cats does the breeder have? How many litters do those cats produce in a year? How many different breeds of kittens does the breeder produce? Why does the breeder choose to sell to pet shops rather than directly to the public? In addition, the prospective buyer should call the humane association in the town where the breeder lives to ask if the breeder enjoys a good reputation in that community.

Recommending this sort of caution is not to insinuate that buying from a pet store is, per se, always more risky than buying directly from a breeder. What is implied, however, is that the buyer should find out as much as possible about a kitten's background no matter where that kitten is acquired.

Pet stores also sell nonpedigreed kittens. These kittens are commonly

obtained from persons in the area whose females had unexpected litters. Anyone buying a nonpedigreed kitten from a pet store should ask the same questions that he or she would ask if the kitten were pedigreed.

The young of any species radiate innocence. Some would say that no other species radiates it as well as kittens do.

Chapter 3
Purebred Personality Myths

Nothing decorates a basket like a kitten—unless it's two kittens.

There are nearly 50 breeds of cats eligible to be registered in one or more of the seven cat associations in North America. Only a fool or a writer on assignment would believe—or try to make you believe—that each one of those breeds has its own separate and distinct personality. Nevertheless, every time a new cat book, magazine, show guide, or series of breed brochures is published, out come the same old formulas with a few scrambled similes tossed in for seasoning. Thus, we are told that

Abyssinians and Somalis can weave between objects like a skier on a slalom course. Oh yeah? Have you ever watched skiers on a slalom course? They hit the poles, you know. Can you imagine that sort of interaction between your downhill Somali and your porcelain cat figurines? Unless your knick-knacks are spring mounted on your windowsill or wherever it is they live, you had better caution your Abyssinian to stay off the slopes.

It probably is easier to navigate a slalom course on a 90° degree slope in a whiteout than it is to work up close to 50 distinct breed-personality sketches. Yet that does not stop people from trying. In one cat federation's Siamese brochure, for example, the Siamese personality is not only an archetype unto itself, it is even subdivided by colors: seal points are extroverts; blue points are loyal and extra affectionate; lilacs are prima donnas; and chocolates are fun loving. Unfortunately, the association in question recognizes Siamese in only four colors. Other associations recognize Siamese in dozens of additional colors. One is

Nothing decorates a basket like a kitten—unless it's two kittens.

left to wonder, therefore, what the differences between the personalities of a seal tortie lynx point Siamese and a chocolate tortie lynx point Siamese might be.

Early Breed Descriptions

Writers have been analyzing cats' behavior—and making breed-specific simplifications—for more than a hundred years. In 1889, six years before Freud got around to publishing *Studies of Hysteria,* Harrison Weir, the Englishman who established the cat fancy, declared that Siamese were widely different from other shorthair cats in "form, color, texture [and] shortness" of coat. Yet, said Weir, "there is but little difference in [the Siamese] mode of life or habit."

However, another Siamese fancier in Weir's chapter reported that her cats were "very affectionate and personally attached to their human friends, not liking to be left alone, and following us from room to room more after the manner of dogs than cats." Do we conclude from this disparity that Weir was misinformed about Siamese? Or that all Victorian-era Siamese cats were doglike in their affection for their owners? Or that Weir did not like Siamese breeders because they went around telling people not to buy his book because he believed too strongly in animal

This Siamese is the kitten most likely to have been on the other end of the line when E.T. phoned home.

rights? Or that vast, intramural differences in personality exist in every breed, even one as distinctive as the Siamese?

Modern-day Delusions

Siamese are not the only cats that suffer from split personalities at the hands of writers. One modern-day cat book announces that a Persian "does not usually wrap itself around its owner's neck or nuzzle." We still have not figured out where one's nuzzle is located, but while nuzzling over that question, we were even more distracted when we read in another cat book that a Persian "generally *does* wrap its paws around [its] owner's neck." (And around its owner's nuzzle as well?) Once again, different observers see different personality traits in the same breed. Therefore, when a person declares that a certain breed of cat is friendly, intelligent, likes to swim, or whatever, what that person is really saying is that the members of the breed he or she has known have been intelligent, friendly, or have liked to swim.

Perhaps having been once nuzzled, Weir was twice shy. He managed close to a thousand words about Manx cats without saying they were quiet, affectionate, gentle, sensitive, intelligent, stubborn, made excellent companions, or needed discipline—as present-day writers have said. Indeed, Weir offered as much information about the Manx personality as a Manx has a tail.

Weir had nothing to say about the personalities of Angora cats, either, whom modern writers have described as courteous, affectionate, gentle, responsive, intelligent, polite, fond of water, and willing to fetch things for their owners. Or about Abyssinians, currently described as active, gentle, affectionate, friendly, inquisitive, quiet, intelligent cats that love to climb, sunbathe, get themselves wet, and fetch things for their owners, but who hate being caged.

The Aby is one of a handful of breeds about which this last point has been made. Are we to infer that all other cats enjoy—or at least do not mind—being caged? We have never interviewed a normal cat that did not hate being caged. Cats were not meant to spend long periods of time in a cage. What is there to do in a cage but pace, sleep, eat, or sulk? We have talked to several breeders who swear their cats do not mind being caged because "they sleep all day anyway," but you would expect somebody who keeps cats in cages most of the time to say a thing like that. Besides, if a cat sleeps all day, why

There is often more myth than meaning in descriptions of cats' personalities.

not let it sleep in a nice, warm window in the sun? Are Abyssinians the only cats that worship the sun? Or is this trait peculiar to the Abys that hate being caged? Our experience has indicated that on a warm afternoon most any cat turns into a four-legged sundial.

Cymrics and Horses?

Without putting too fine a point or too many synonyms on the issue, we have found that most writers do quite nicely describing cat breeds from Abyssinian to Japanese bobtail. At about the dozenth breed, writers hit the thesaurus. At two dozen they hit the bottle. And at three dozen they hit the wall. Thus we find people saying that Korats have a strong sense of time and place; cymrics are excellent with horses; Chartreux smile frequently and love large dogs; Burmese can perform headstands; Havanas raise their paws in greeting; and the Birman appears conscious of its sacred origin.

We drew the line and the covers at that one. First of all, the sacred origin of Birmans (guardians of the temple, changed miraculously from solid white to a Himalayan pattern, and so on) is a sacred myth. What's more, we have firsthand knowledge of cats that were born in the house in which they currently reside, and these cats are emphatically unaware of their origin. Of course, it was not a sacred origin. Does that make a difference?

Personality and Coat Length

Lest anyone think we mean to imply that cats have no personality, we do not. Nor do we mean to imply that the ancients were silent on the matter. Witness the following from Weir: "I am of the opinion that the short-haired cat in general is of a more genial temperament, more 'cossetty,' more observant, more quick in adapting itself to its surroundings and circumstances than its long-haired brother.

"At the same time I am willing to admit," Weir continued, "that some of these peculiarities being set aside, the long-haired cat is charmingly beautiful, and at the same time has a large degree of intelligence—in fact much more than most animals that I know, not even setting aside the dog, and I have come to this conclusion after much long, careful, and mature consideration."

Personality and Body Type

Weir was onto something there, but personality does not shake out along coat-length dimensions as he thought it did. Some observers suspect that personality is not so much

A Siamese mother relaxes with a kitten that is not much more awake than she is.

A Devon rex coming to terms with its world—and seemingly determined to bend the world to its terms.

This Balinese mother watches while her trusting kittens meditate.

A Japanese bobtail kitten voicing an appeal for attention.

a function of coat length—or even breed—as it is a function of body type. Cobby-bodied, endomorphic cats are complacent; tubular, ectomorphic cats are tireless; and anything in between is anybody's guess.

Trouble is, most cat breeds—all but about six or seven to be exact—were recognized after 1950. Some breeders take longer than 40 years to grow a personality. Imagine how long a breed must take. Furthermore, there have been few if any scientific inquiries into the personality differences between cat breeds. Authors may cite surveys of university undergraduates, cat show judges, or veterinarians, but the

These Persian kittens are about to weigh in with their theory of purebred-cat personality.

Norwegian Forest kittens exploring the great indoors.

A Maine Coon kitten trying to put its nose back into joint.

British shorthair kittens feeling quite at home—thank you—on a Victorian chair.

resulting anecdotes gathered cannot take the place of scientific, verifiable studies.

Until a more rigorous analysis comes along, we would make bold to suggest that there are three feline personalities: Siamese (ecto-morph), Persian (endomorph), and in between (mesomorph).

The Siamese personality (ecto-morph) group includes Siamese, colorpoint shorthairs, Oriental shorthairs, Oriental longhairs, Bali-nese, Javanese, Abyssinians, Somali, Cornish rex, Devon rex, Turkish Angoras, Japanese bob-tails, and Sphynx. Generally, and perhaps even commonly, these

An Egyptian mau mouths a toy mouse.

A Manx kitten is ineffably soft, unerringly cute, unfailingly mischievous, and surprisingly resilient.

"Vase? What vase? We don't see any vase," say these Tonkinese innocents.

These ocicats demonstrate that spots and stripes can coexist peacefully.

cats are more active, vocal, intelligent, inquisitive, and occasionally exasperating than are cats in the other personality groups.

The Persian personality (endomorph) group includes Persians, ragdolls, Birman, Chartreux, British shorthairs, Kashmir, Maine coon cats, Norwegian forest cats, and Himalayans. These breeds are considerably more sedentary, less

vocal, more ground based, less intelligent for the most part, and not as likely to get into mischief as are Siamese personality cats.

The mesomorph group includes Singapuras, Turkish vans, Egyptian maus, Bengals, Burmese, foreign Burmese, Bombays, Havana browns, ocicats, tonkinese, snowshoes, Korats, Manx, cymrics, Russian blues, American shorthairs,

American wirehairs, American curls, Scottish folds, longhair Scottish folds, and exotic shorthairs.

Easily the most variable of the three personality groups, mesomorphs are also the group about which it is most foolhardy to generalize, for characteristics overlap considerably between individual members of the breeds in this group. For example, the exotic shorthair was created from crosses between Persians and various shorthair breeds, mostly American shorthairs. Not surprisingly, the exotic has a vertical leap and a disposition somewhere between the Persian and the American shorthair, but among exotic shorthairs you will find cats that are quite active and cats that are quite sedentary.

If cat personalities are arranged along a normal curve, mesomorphs would occupy the standard deviations immediately to the right and the left of the mean (average). Siamese personality types would occupy the second and third standard deviations to the right of the mean, and Persian personality types would occupy the second and third standard deviations to the left of the mean.

Socialization and Personality

Although temperament is heritable to a slight degree, the way a kitten is raised is more important in shaping its personality. Kittens that are not handled often enough between the ages of three and fourteen weeks are less likely to develop into well-adjusted family members than are kittens that receive frequent handling and attention. Therefore, it is well to ask how many litters a breeder produces each year and how many other litters he or she was raising when the kitten in which you are interested was growing up. A breeder who produces more than two or three litters a year—or who was raising several other litters while your kitten's litter was maturing—may not have had time to socialize every kitten in those litters properly. A breeder who raises one or two litters at a time has more opportunity to give each of those kittens the individual attention it deserves. In general, the smaller the cattery, the more user-friendly the kittens it will produce. And user-friendly is the best personality type of all.

Chapter 4
Choosing the Right Kitten

No matter where you obtain a kitten—once you have decided that a kitten is the right companion for you—there are certain questions to consider: Do you want a male or a female? One kitten or two? Are you interested in showing or breeding? Do you want a longhair or a shorthair? An active kitten or one that is more sedate? Like people, kittens come in a variety of personalities and body styles, from shy to scintillating, from stocky to svelte. Your own disposition, your personal taste, and your living arrangements will determine what sort of kitten is best for you.

These kittens are on a field trip that is part of the Introduction to the Big World seminar.

First Considerations

Sex

Although some people may prefer male or female cats as pets, either sex—if given love, attention, and a warm bed to sleep in at night (preferably yours)—will make a devoted companion. You will pay one third to one half more to spay a female than you will to neuter a male, and neutered males, as they grow older, should not be fed a diet with a mineral composition that will produce an alkaline rather than an acidic urine. Otherwise there is no difference in the cost associated with—or the care required in—keeping an altered male or female in the manner to which either would like to become accustomed.

Cost

The price of a kitten or cat is determined by quality, supply, demand, and geography. Many kittens do not cost anything more than the price of a veterinary inspection to obtain. These are the free-to-good-home kittens advertised in newspapers, on bulletin boards at veterinarians' offices, and on telephone poles at the end of driveways. Also "free" are the kittens that adopt you, turning up on your doorstep with a lean and hungry and entirely fetching look.

Only slightly more expensive are nonpedigreed kittens sold in pet shops and kittens adopted from animal shelters. Nonpedigreed kittens in pet shops usually cost from $9.99 to $29.99, seldom more. Kittens adopted in shelters cost $50 or so, depending on the extras that come with the kitten. Those extras can include the kitten's first shots and an examination by a veterinarian. Prices for pedigreed kittens are higher than for any other kind. Some newspapers carry classified ads that offer pedigreed kittens for as little as $75 to $150. Most breeders, however, charge somewhat more for a pet-quality kitten, usually $300 or $400. Exotic breeds will be even more costly.

The purchase price is not the only cost encountered when buying a kitten. You also will have to pay for a veterinary inspection (a prudent investment even if the kitten has been examined before you acquire it) and, perhaps, for any additional vaccinations the kitten may require. Furthermore, if you buy a pedigreed kitten from a breeder who lives beyond driving distance, you will have to pay to have the kitten shipped by plane. Shipping costs vary with the length of the flight, the method of shipping, and the airline involved. Kittens can be shipped on short flights for $30 to $40. Transcontinental journeys can cost $100 or more.

You also must pay for the carrier in which the kitten is shipped. Carriers that conform to airline specifications can be purchased at cat shows, pet shops, or some airline cargo offices. A secure, durable carrier costs $25 to $35, depending on its size.

One Kitten or Two?

If you are away during the day and you have no other pets with which your kitten can socialize while your are gone, you should consider getting two kittens that are roughly the same age. Not only will you

The kitten in the carrier is about to discover that there is a paw at the end of the tunnel.

double your pleasure by watching two kittens playing instead of one, but kittens are less apt to be bored or lonely if they have another kitten to talk to when you are not at home.

Show Cat or Pet?

If you are buying a pedigreed cat, you want a pet-quality kitten, unless you are planning to show or breed that cat. Pet-quality—a hapless and somewhat snobbish-sounding term—is applied to kittens with some cosmetic disadvantage that would compromise their breeding or showing success. Pet-quality cats may have eyes that are not as large as a show cat's eyes or a nose that is a bit too long or too short or a muzzle that is not round enough nor square enough, or some other "fault" or minor accumulation of faults.

If you are interested in showing but the idea of raising kittens does not appeal to you at all, you should look for a show-quality kitten anyway. Many breeders will gladly sell show-quality kittens to persons who will allow the kittens the run of the house, have them altered when they are of a certain age, and show them in adult classes for altered cats.

Basic Personality Tests

To get a reading of a kitten's personality, simply flutter a few fingers along the floor about 6 inches (15.2

cm) in front of the kitten or drag a small toy back and forth about the same distance away. Does the kitten rush to investigate? Does it back away in fright? Or does it scamper under the nearest sofa?

Well-adjusted, healthy kittens exhibit a robust curiosity about fingers, toys, and anything else that moves within sight. Kittens that are nervous or timid or not feeling well are more cautious upon meeting strangers. Poorly adjusted kittens take cover under the nearest chair.

If you have other pets or children at home, the inquisitive, pleased-to-meet-you kitten is the best choice. The timid kitten may well make a good companion, too; but it may take longer to adjust, and is, perhaps, better off with experienced cat owners who have no pets or young children currently. And the little pair of eyes under the chair? Shy kittens need love, too. Lots of it. If you have no other pets or if you

infectious. A kitten with pale gums may be anemic. If its ears are waxy inside, that may only be a sign of neglect; but if the ears are caked with dirt, the kitten may have ear mites. If a kitten's ribs are protruding or if it is potbellied, it may be undernourished or it may have worms. A kitten with a dull coat or a coat that is dotted with scabs, tiny specks of dirt, or bald spots may have ringworm (a highly transmissible fungal infection) or fleas. A kitten with wet hindquarters may develop urine scalding; if they are dirty, it may have diarrhea. Both urine scalding and diarrhea are signs of poor health.

Kittens always hit their marks when it's time to strike a pose.

plan to acquire two kittens at once—and if you have the time and patience required to nurture such a reluctant flower—more power to you. If not, perhaps the next person who comes along will be the right owner for this needy kitten.

A Good Health Inventory

A healthy kitten's eyes are bright, shiny, and clear. Its nose is cool and a bit damp. Its gums are neither pale nor inflamed. Its ears are free of wax or dirt. Its body is soft and smooth, a little lean perhaps, but not skinny. Its coat is clean and free of bald patches, scabs, or tiny specks of black dirt. The area around its tail is not dirty or discolored.

A kitten with runny eyes may be in poor health. Inflamed gums may indicate a variety of causes, nutritional or

What a work ethic—nursing one kitten and cleaning another at the same time!

Three kittens practicing the look of wary surprise. The kitten on the left does not yet have the look down pat.

How Old Is Old Enough?

Kittenhood is one of the most enjoyable aspects of owning a cat. Cats are cats virtually their entire lives, but they are kittens for only a few cherished months, and new owners are understandably keen to take their kittens home as soon as possible. Nonetheless, responsible breeders, pet shops, or shelters do not sell or place kittens until they are 12 weeks old. (Regrettably, most states allow kittens to be sold or adopted as soon as they are eight weeks old.)

By the time a kitten is 12 weeks old, it has been weaned properly, has been eating solid food for several weeks, and is on its little way to becoming a mature cat. What's more, a 12-week-old kitten has had most, if not all, of its distemper series vaccinations.

Kittens that are six to ten weeks old are still infants. If you take them away from their mothers and their siblings at that tender age, the stress of adjusting to new surroundings may cause kittens to become sick, to forget their litter training, or to "nurse" on blankets or sofa cushions—a habit they may never outgrow. No matter how much you are tempted by an eight-week-old kitten, it will adjust better—and you will be doing it a favor—if it is allowed to remain in its original home until it is 12 weeks old.

Foundling kittens often are separated from their mothers before the kittens are 12 weeks old. In this case, you should not reject the kitten because it is so young, but you should lavish extra attention on it to make up for the maternal affection it has been denied.

Buying a Show Cat

Persons interested in buying a show cat and in breeding their own cats should start with the best quality female they can find. They also should remember that quality is not always proportionate to price and that registration papers merely indicate that a cat is eligible to be registered, not that it is good enough to be shown. Any registered cat can be entered in a show, but there is a measurable difference between a cat that can be shown and a show cat. The former is a serviceable and decorative zircon, the latter is a genuine diamond—often of great price.

It is even more difficult for a novice to evaluate a kitten's show potential than to gauge its personality and general state of health. An encrusted eye is an encrusted eye to most observers, but eyes of the correct size, shape, and setting are more difficult for a novice to identify, and the difficulty is compounded because kittens have yet to finish maturing.

That is why a journey of hundreds of dollars (or more) must begin with a few basic steps: visit shows, talk to breeders, watch classes being judged, and learn what winning cats of various breeds look like. Talk to judges when they have finished judging and ask them to recommend one or two breeders who work with the breed or breeds in which you are interested. If possible, visit several breeders who are willing to spend an afternoon or evening discussing cats with you and using their own cats to illustrate the fine points of the breed.

Most important, study the breed standard(s) for the breed(s) you are considering buying. Take a copy of the standard along when you go to look at kittens, and ask breeders to point out where a kitten or a cat meets the standard and where it does not. If the breeder does not object, take an experienced breeder along when you go to look at kittens.

Breeders with the best available kittens will not always live within driving distance, so you may have nothing more on which to make an

A ruddy Abyssinian who has just discovered that dinner is going to be late.

informed decision than a few pictures and the breeder's evaluation of the kitten in which you are interested. If the pictures are fuzzy, ask to see more. If you have any grounds for doubting the breeder's word, look for another breeder. In any event, ask the breeder to say, preferably in writing, where a kitten measures up to the standard and where that kitten is lacking. Breeders usually will not guarantee a kitten's performance in the show ring, but a breeder should be willing to say whether a kitten looks like best-in-show material or a top-ten finalist and roughly how many shows the kitten will take, after it grows up, to earn the titles offered by the various cat associations.

Anyone buying a show kitten is also buying a conglomeration of genes that kitten has inherited from its ancestors. The names and titles of the first four or five generations of ancestors are recorded on a

This Persian, like all cats, was born to sleep. There is nothing else they do so copiously or so well.

cat's pedigree. Buyers should study a pedigree to see what titles the members of a kitten's family have won—especially its parents and grandparents, for the first two generations have the greatest impact on a kitten's development.

The most meaningful title awarded in the show ring by most associations is that of grand champion. The more grand champions recorded in the first two or three generations of a kitten's pedigree, the better its ancestors have done in competition, and the better its chances, theoretically at least, of living up to the family tradition.

Some kittens never look anything but smashing from an early age, but the average youngster goes through several stages while it is growing up—from caterpillar to butterfly and sometimes back again. You should wait, therefore, until a potential show-quality kitten is five or six months old before you buy it. A five- or six-month-old kitten is less subject to change without notice than is a younger kitten. Besides, a kitten that has reached that age has been shown a time or two perhaps.

Papers and Contracts

Breeders should provide a sales contract (see page 124) when selling a kitten. Most contracts specify the price of the kitten, the amount of the deposit required to hold the kitten, if any, when the balance of the payment is due, and so on. Contracts also may specify that if at any time the buyer no longer can keep the kitten—or no longer wishes to keep it—the breeder must be given an opportunity to buy the kitten back at the going rate for kittens or cats at that time. Finally, a contract should allow a new owner a definite period of time, usually three to five working days, in which to take a kitten to a veterinarian for an examination. If the vet discovers any preexisting conditions such as leukemia or feline infectious peritonitis, you should have the right to return the kitten at the seller's expense and to have the purchase price refunded.

If you give a breeder a deposit on a kitten, you should write "deposit for thus-and-such kitten" on the memo line of the check. You should make a similar notation when writing a check for the balance of the payment. Expect to be given a receipt for all payments and find out in advance—and in writing if you wish—whether a deposit is refundable should you decide not to take the kitten. Remember, too, that once a breeder has accepted money or some other consideration in return for reserving a kitten for you, that breeder has entered into an option contract; and he or she cannot legally revoke or renegotiate the offer—as some breeders have been known to do—if the kitten turns out to be much better than the breeder had anticipated.

Be sure to read a contract meticulously before signing it because contracts are legally binding once they have been signed by both parties. If a contract contains any stipulations that you do not understand or do not wish to agree to—like a stipulation saying that the cat can never be declawed—you should discuss these issues with the breeder before signing.

In addition to the pedigree, new owners may receive "papers" when they buy a pedigreed cat. These papers usually consist of a registration slip that the new owner can fill out and send—along with the required $6 or $7 fee—to the administrative office of the association in which that kitten's litter has been registered. The association then returns a certificate of ownership to the new owners.

Anyone who buys a kitten or a cat that already has been registered by its breeder will receive an owner's certificate. On the back of that certificate is a transfer-of-ownership section that must be signed by the breeder and the new owner. Once the required signatures are present, the new owner mails the certificate, with the appropriate transfer fee, to the administrative office of the association in which the cat has been registered. The association will send back a new, amended certificate of ownership to the new owner(s).

Many breeders will not provide a registration slip to anyone who buys a pet-quality kitten until they receive proof that the kitten has been neutered or spayed. Some breeders do not supply registration slips on pet-quality kittens at all. Breeders withhold papers to prevent unscrupulous people from buying a kitten at a pet price and then breeding it and to prevent the use of pet-quality kittens in breedings that have virtually no chance of contributing to the aesthetic improvement of a breed.

Health Certificates

The most important documents that accompany a kitten to its new home are health records and vaccination certificates. You should not accept a kitten without these papers. Some breeders, especially those who produce a large number of kittens, economize by giving vaccinations themselves. There is nothing illegal about this practice, yet there is more to immunizing a kitten than drawing vaccine into a syringe, inserting the needle under a kitten's skin, and pushing the plunger. Few, if any, breeders are capable of examining a kitten as thoroughly as a veterinarian can before administering a vaccination. Indeed, a vaccination is only as good as the examination that precedes it. This examination is important because vaccine given to a sick kitten will do more harm than good. Thus, a kitten should be examined by a veterinarian at least once before it is sold, preferably before its first vaccination. Finally, all kittens being shipped by air should be accompanied by a health certificate issued by a veterinarian and by a certificate verifying that a kitten has received all the vaccinations required by the city or state to which the kitten is being shipped.

Chapter 5
Living With a New Kitten

For many people shopping is a cross between a religion, an art form, an irresistible impulse, a therapeutic exercise, a declaration of self, and a near clinical preoccupation. These same descriptors apply to the emotional relationship that many people have to cats. What could be more compelling, then, for persons in the subset formed by the intersection of the oniophile group (those who love to shop) and the ailurophile group (those who love cats) than to go shopping for kitten supplies? The following suggestions are offered as a public service to new kitten owners.

A Shopping List for New Owners

Litter pan: Litter pans come in a variety of styles and colors. Some pans are open; some are enclosed; some are outfitted with raised, detachable rims, and some enclosed pans are equipped with an opera window so that cat owners can tell—without having to lift the top—whether or not a pan needs cleaning.

Enclosed pans and those with detachable rims are designed to keep the litter in the pan when kittens get to digging. No matter what style of pan your cats prefer, however, litter pans should be at least 19 inches (48 cm) by 15 inches (38.1 cm) by 4 inches (10 cm) deep and should be made of sturdy, washable material.

Litter: All litter, whether its composition is absorbent in varying degrees, but no litter is entirely "dust" free. The finer the grains of litter, the more likely they are to get kicked out of the pan, especially if the pan is not enclosed or fitted with a detachable rim.

Litter is also subject to sticking between a kitten's toes and falling out around the house. To solve this problem, several pet-supply manufacturers sell pads that are designed to spread a kitten's toes gently as soon as it steps out of the litter pan, thereby releasing any toe-jammed litter onto the pad instead of the furniture or rugs.

Many people prefer litter that forms clumps when a kitten urinates on it. Other kitten owners favor deodorant litter, which is specially scented to mask litter pan odors. One recently marketed litter changes color as the pH of a kitten's urine changes from alkaline to acid or vice versa.

Litter scoop: The sturdier the scoop, the longer it survives, but always have a spare in reserve just in case.

Litter pan liners: Liners are not always practical for day-to-day use at home because the more frequently kittens use a pan, the more frequently litter pan liners are punctured by kittens' claws. Liners can be convenient, nevertheless, for bundling up the contents of the pan and discarding them during motel stays.

Age does have its prerogatives, as this mother cat is demonstrating at the food bowl.

Food dishes and water bowls: Food dishes and water bowls should be made of glass, ceramic, or metal. Reusable plastic can

retain odors even if washed carefully. Disposable plastic is a burden on the environment. All dishes and bowls should be solid and heavy enough not to tip over easily. If made of glass, they should be sturdy enough not to break, crack, or chip when a kitten knocks them over.

Place mats: Whether made of plain rubber or glossy vinyl decorated with cute kitten faces, place mats will protect the floor underneath food dishes and water bowls.

Scratching post: A scratching post spares the furniture while providing kittens with an acceptable outlet for exercising their natural instinct to scratch. The post should be well anchored, so that it will not tip over when it is used, and it should be tall enough so that as kittens mature they can stretch while

scratching. The scratching surface should be made of sisal or hemp or some other hardy, resilient material. Floor-to-ceiling scratching posts with shelves on which kittens can sit ought to be especially well anchored and secure.

Padded window perches: Once kittens are old enough to jump onto window sills, padded window perches can transform a window with a narrow, cramped sill into a comfortable observation deck. Most perches can be clamped easily to the wall.

Grooming tools: Kittens are naturally fastidious, but supplementary grooming by their owners should be part of all kittens' routines. Pet shops, animal-supply houses, many veterinary offices, and vendors at cat shows carry shampoos, nail clippers, brushes, combs, powders, ointments, and sprays for your kitten's beautification. (See The Right Tools, page 78.)

Toys: A dazzling assortment of toys, each contrived to afford your kitten endless hours of fun, is available from pet shops, animal-supply houses, and vendors at cat shows; but flash and fun should not be the main criteria used in selecting toys for a kitten. Toys must be safe as well as seductive. Balls with bells inside should be sturdy enough so that a kitten cannot dig the bell out and swallow it. Eyes, noses, and all appendages on small, stuffed mice and other prey substitutes should be virtually welded on for the same reason—as should streamers and any

other attachments on toys. Before buying a toy for your kitten, imagine how that toy could cause harm. If there is any possibility that it could, it probably will. Don't buy it.

For all their fuss and feathers, store-bought toys are not the only games in town. Kittens will amuse themselves mightily with a crumpled piece of paper, an empty film

Did this cat just hear a door open? Will this cat be racing from its padded window perch before you can turn the page?

A kitten fears no toy, no matter how large its head or how long its tail.

canister, a cardboard box turned upside down with holes cut at either end, or a plain, brown paper grocery bag. (Indeed, some companies now manufacture sacks that sound like paper bags when kittens explore them.)

The same cautions expressed about store-bought toys apply to the homemade kind. They should not be decorated with dangling strings for kittens to get tangled up in or to swallow. They should not contain bits or pieces that kittens can chew off and eat. Nor should they have sharp edges on which kittens could get hurt. Neither should kittens be allowed to play with cellophane, plastic wrap, aluminum foil, twist ties from sandwich and garbage bags, rubber bands, or cotton swabs.

Beds: Many kittens are inclined to disdain elaborate, costly beds and to settle down instead in a cozy window, a comfortable chair, or on their owners' pillows. Before buying a kitten bed, wait until your kitten has chosen a spot in which to sleep, then buy a bed to fit that spot and to make it even more comfortable.

Cat carrier: You will need a safe, sturdy carrier in which to bring your kitten home for the first time, to take your kitten to the veterinarian for checkups, and, perhaps, for vacations and travel. A good carrier, besides having a secure handle and door latch, should be well ventilated and washable. Heavy-molded plastic carriers are the best choice. They can be purchased at pet shops, from animal-supply houses, at cat shows, and from some airline cargo offices.

Food: Most supermarkets, convenience stores, pet shops, or feed stores—and a number of veterinary offices—carry a plentiful choice of foods to suit a kitten's palate and nutritional needs. Whichever of the hundreds of brands or varieties you select, it should provide 100 percent-complete nutrition for growth or for all stages of a cat's life, and the label should say so. Do not give your kitten food that is intended for the maintenance of adult cats only. (See The Well-fed Kitten, page 45.)

Kitten-proofing Your House

Kittens combine a two-year-old's sense of curiosity and restraint with a teenager's athletic ability. If there

A Persian kitten about to indulge in holiday temptations makes a pretty picture, but one that is potentially hazardous.

are rooms in your house that you do not want your kitten to investigate, keep the doors to those rooms closed. If there are breakable objects in the rooms your kitten is allowed to visit, put them out of reach. Make sure all balconies are enclosed, all window screens are secured, and all electrical cords are intact. If your kitten begins teething on electrical cords, wrap them in heavy tape or cover them with plastic tubes, which you can buy in an auto-supply shop. If necessary, unplug all appliances that are not in use until you are certain your kitten has not developed a taste for electrical cords. To keep your kitten from getting a charge out of electrical sockets, cover them with plastic, plug-in socket guards, which you can buy at the hardware store.

Keep all kitchen and bathroom cleansers, chemicals, cleaners, and toilet articles in cabinets that cannot be pried open by inquisitive kittens. Keep the lids on all trash containers tightly closed. Consider replacing trash receptacles whose swing-open lids could be dislodged if your kitten overturns the containers. (Another lid to keep down is the toilet seat lid, especially if you use an automatic-release cleaning product.)

When closing any door in your house—the front door, back door, refrigerator door, closet door, the door on the clothes washer or dryer—be sure your kitten is not on the wrong side. Keep the bathroom

door closed when you are filling the tub. When cleaning, rinse all cleansers and chemicals thoroughly from any surfaces on which a kitten might walk. What gets on a kitten's paws has a way of getting into a kitten's stomach.

Gather up sewing supplies and yarn when you are finished using them and put them safely away. Do not leave rubber bands, hot irons, cigarettes, plastic bags, or pieces of string lying around. Beware, also, of tinsel and other decorations on a Christmas tree, a dangling tablecloth, and a hot burner on the stove.

All outside doors—and balcony doors, too—should be closed securely at all times. Screen doors, even when they are closed, present a challenge to growing kittens, who often carve out their own cat flaps in them. Wooden or wrought iron latticework installed over screen doors is both decorative and protective.

Before you bring your kitten home for the first time, take a slow,

Besides looking out of windows, cats sometimes look for a way out of windows.

meditative walk through your house. Try to think like a curious, mischief-prone kitten when you do. Imagine all the places where calamity might lurk, waiting for a kitten to make it happen.

Plants to Leaf Alone

Many beautiful, harmless-looking plants are capable of producing illness or death in kittens. Pernicious plants can be grouped according to the effect they produce in animals: gastrointestinal, cardiovascular, nervous system, and irritation or mechanical. The safest way to enjoy

Before you buy that kitten, make sure none of your houseplants can do it any harm.

your kitten is by hanging your plants well out of your kitten's reach.

Plants that are harmful to kittens do not live only indoors. If you decide to allow your kitten to go outside—a decision that should not be made lightly—make sure there are no dangerous plants in your garden.

Plants with gastrointestinal effects: amaryllis, azalea, bittersweet, bird of paradise, black locust, buckeye (horse chestnut), castor bean, common box, daffodil, daphne, English ivy, eggplant, euonymus, four-o'clock, ground cherry, holly, honeysuckle, hyacinth, iris (flag), jasmine, Jerusalem cherry, lords and ladies, mock orange, mushrooms, potato, privet, spurges, rain tree (monkeypod), rhododendron, sandbox tree, wisteria, yellow allamdanda, yew.

Plants with cardiovascular effects: anconite, foxglove, larkspur, lily of the valley, monkshood, oleander, yellow oleander, yew.

Plants with nervous system effects: angel's trumpet, almond, apple, apricot, belladonna, bleeding heart, cardinal flower, cherry, chinaberry tree, deadly nightshade, Dutchman's-breeches, elderberry, goldenchain tree, henbane, hydrangea, jasmine, jimsonweed, Kentucky coffee tree, lantana, marijuana, mescal bean, moonseed, morning glory, peach, periwinkle, thorn apple, tobacco, tree tobacco, yellow jasmine.

Plants that produce irritation or mechanical injury: barleys, blackberry, bromegrasses, burdock, cacti, caladium, calla lily, Carolina nightshade, cocklebur, dumbcane (dieffenbachia), elephant's ear, foxtail, goathead, jack-in-the-pulpit, needlegrass, nettle, poinsettia, philodendron, pyracantha, sandbur, snow-on-the-mountain, spurge, triple awn.

Kitten's First Impressions

You have located every item on your shopping list and have discovered a few extra toys as well. You have washed the litter pan, filled it with 1.5 to 2 inches (3.8–5 cm) of litter, and placed it in a quiet location away from the areas where your kitten is going to eat or sleep. You have made a final safety check of the house. At last, it is time to bring your new kitten home.

If you work during the week, schedule homecoming for the start of a weekend or a holiday; and remember that even though you have planned carefully for this day and have thought about little else for some time, it will come as a major surprise to your kitten. Chances are it will be leaving its mother, its playmates, its people, or a home to which it has grown accustomed. Some kittens adjust swimmingly. After they are taken from their carriers and are placed in their new litter pans, they look

around as if to say, "Nice digs. When's dinner?"

Other kittens are not so self-assured. Do not be alarmed if your kitten looks uneasy at first or looks around and scurries under the sofa. Pour a cup of coffee or some other beverage, pull up a chair, and turn on the television or read the newspaper. If you select the right channel, the tranquil sounds will have a calming effect on your kitten. Eventually your new pet's curiosity will overwhelm it. No kitten has ever refused permanently to come out from under a sofa. Once the underside of the sofa has been mastered, your kitten will be ready to take the measure of additional areas in your house. You will have plenty of time to make the kitten's acquaintance then.

Kittens should be raised with people underfoot.

Your kitten will feel more snug in its new home if there is something from its former home on hand: a favorite toy, a blanket or a bed, a preferred food, even a small amount of soiled litter scattered in the new pan. These items give off familiar, comforting smells that are reassuring in a strange setting.

Introducing Other Pets

You should be cautious when introducing a kitten to other four-legged members of the family. The chances of hostilities breaking out vary directly with the age and tenure of the cat or dog already in residence. If you have an eight-year-old pet that always has been an only child, you probably should not get a new kitten. If your pet is four years old or younger, you should be able to introduce a new kitten if you manage the introduction carefully—and if you keep in mind how you would feel if a stranger suddenly was brought to your house for an indefinite stay without anyone consulting you first.

Again, bring the new kitten home on a weekend or a holiday. Before you do, prepare a room where the newcomer will spend some time in isolation. Do not select the old cat's favorite sanctuary or resting place for this purpose. The idea is to fit the new kitten into the old cat's routine without making the old cat feel threatened.

Solitary confinement is recommended for the kitten, no matter how current the old cat's vaccinations are or how well the kitten passed the veterinary exam. Until you are satisfied that the kitten is not harboring any illnesses that did not show up during the vet inspection—that is, for ten days to two weeks—it should have no direct and extended contact with the old cat. The kitten should, of course, have plenty of visits from you, and you should disinfect your hands thoroughly after each visit.

For the first couple of days allow the cats to sniff, and perhaps to hiss, at each other from either side of a closed door. To be sure, infectious diseases can be spread by this sort of incidental contact—and some diseases are airborne—but isolation will curtail the spread of infections that occur primarily when

"My, my, Puppy Dog, what big ears you have."

cats use the same litter pan, eat or drink from the same bowl, and lick or bite each other. Thus, the isolation advice is given in the belief that half an ounce of protection is better than none.

When you sense that the time is right—and after you have clipped the kitten's and the old cat's claws—put the kitten into a cat carrier, open the door to the room, and allow the old cat in for a five- to ten-minute visit. Be sure to take up the kitten's water bowl, food dish, and litter pan first.

Repeat these daily visits until the cats are no longer hissing, growling, or arching their backs at one another; then allow the cats free-ranging, but supervised, contact. Bring the old cat into the isolation room, but this time do not confine the kitten beforehand. Put the old cat on the floor, retire to a neutral corner, and have a blanket, a pan of cold water, and a broom handy. All should go well, but if the rare, life-threatening fight breaks out, use the pan of water and/or the broom to separate the combatants, and throw the blanket over the nearest one. While the cat is wriggling around beneath the blanket, scoop up both the blanket and the cat and return the latter to its original territory.

After a day or so, begin the brief visitations again. A few days after that, try the free-range introduction once more. Do not stew if the cats refuse to cozy up together in a corner. The best they may attain is a distant but tolerant relationship.

The guidelines for introducing a kitten to a dog in residence are virtually the same. In addition, if you put a lead on the dog, you should have no trouble separating the animals if necessary. Do not remove the lead until you are sure the participants will not start fighting like cats and dogs. Be especially careful if you have a terrier, a sight hound, a retriever, or any dog that might consider the cat fair game.

A dog that is obviously not familiar with the adage: "Let sleeping cats lie."

When to Have Your Kitten Altered

Unaltered cats are not so easy to live with as are altered cats. Whole males are wont to spray their urine to attract females and to regard any other cat as a potential mate or sparring partner. Females will come into season periodically, a condition accompanied by frequent caterwauling, restlessness, excessive attachment to their owners, occasional spraying of their urine, and an inclination to bolt out of opened doors.

Most breeders and veterinarians suggest that females be altered when they are six months old and males when they are seven to ten months old. At these ages, sexual development is nearly complete, but undesirable traits—spraying by male cats, for example—have not become habits.

A few breeders—and a number of animal shelters—have begun altering kittens before they are 12 weeks old because a few people who buy kittens—and who sign spay-neuter agreements when they do—breed the kittens when they grow up anyway. Obviously, early neutering or spaying prevents this possibility; but it may also cause difficulties when cats grow older. As of this writing, there are no longitudinal studies demonstrating that early neutering or spaying is harmless in the long run.

Licenses, Collars, and ID Tags

Many of the differences between cat and dog behavior can be explained by the differences in the way each species evolved. Dogs are pack animals. Cats are not. Dogs, therefore, are inclined to applaud our actions. Cats instinctively appraise our motivation.

There are differences, too, in the behavior of dog and cat owners. The more one observes these differences, the more one is apt to believe that at some point in their evolution dog owners belonged to pack-dwelling tribes, whereas cat owners resided in single-person households. If this were so, it would help to explain the average cat owner's resistance to the idea of cat licensing. That opposition was expressed grandly by a cat owner in San Francisco who declared: "It is ridiculous to charge a license fee for an animal that is its own creature. We don't choose cats; they choose us. And when they decide to leave, they go."

But, say the advocates of cat licensing, if they are wearing a license on a collar when they go, there is a better chance, if they are found, that they will be returned their owners. Indeed, according to American Humane Association figures for the years 1985 through 1992, 16 percent of all lost dogs were reunited with their owners, but only 2.5 percent of wayward cats were returned to their homes.

"A license is the only form of protection for a pet," says Kim Sturla, companion-animal programs director of The Fund for Animals. "Without one, it's almost impossible to return the animal to its owner."

What's more, animal shelters and pounds in many states will not hold an unlicensed cat as long as they will hold a cat wearing a tag. In some cities, pounds are not required to hold a cat at all, and stray cats not wearing identification are euthanized at once. To a degree, then, licensing would give cats legal recognition and, to some degree, it would give cat owners the right to demand certain considerations because their license fees would generate revenue.

In addition to benefiting the owners of lost cats—not to mention the cats themselves—license fees would allow cat owners to help subsidize shelter activities, which dog owners, through their license fees, have been helping to subsidize for some time.

Originally, the demand for dog-control and dog-licensing laws grew out of the need to protect livestock in rural areas from stray packs of dogs. Because cats did not contribute to this problem, most control and licensing laws were not written to include cats. Moreover, dogs constituted greater health hazards to humans, and they (dogs) remain far more likely to attack humans than do cats; but the increasing popularity of cats and their increasing appearance in animal shelters have led some people to conclude that cats ought to be licensed, too.

Although few states mandate cat licensing—Arkansas, Maryland, Michigan, Oklahoma, and Washington among them—municipalities may require licensing if a state does not; and once cat licensing is estab-lished, differential licensing becomes a possibility. The differential concept is simple and compelling. If it costs $10 to license an altered cat and $50 to license an unaltered one, perhaps more people will get their cats altered. If more people get their cats altered, perhaps fewer litters of kittens will be born. If fewer litters of kittens are born, perhaps fewer unwanted kittens will die in shelters and pounds.

Opponents of steep differential licensing say that it simply will cause honest people to disobey the law by refusing to buy licenses for their unaltered animals, but predictions of lawless behavior are not the criteria by which the worth of a law should be judged. The animal control costs generated by unrestricted breeding are considerable. Those costs, not the possibility that some people will defy a law in order to save a few dollars, are the criteria by which the appropriateness of differential licensing ought to be weighed.

Until recently cats had not been perceived as a rabies threat. That is why rabies vaccinations, mandatory for dogs in virtually every state, are required for cats in fewer than two dozen states. With the increase in the number of rabies cases among cats, however, and with the growth of the cat population in the United States, has come a growing interest in cat licensing as a means of combating rabies. By requiring cat owners to show proof of rabies inoculation before being issued a license for their cats, municipalities hope to increase the number of cats inoculated against rabies.

If there is one thing on which pro- and anti-licensing forces agree, it is this: compliance with cat licensing laws is not going to be swift or universal. "Licensing compliance, in the best of communities, rarely exceeds 40 percent," says one official of The Humane Society of The United States. "Voluntary compliance is usually around 10 percent, and if you patrol regularly, you might get it up to 20, 25 percent. I've never heard of anyone getting beyond 50 percent for licensing compliance."

Be that as it may, say licensing proponents, half a population is better than none.

"Just as I thought. Your name is Terminator."

Chapter 6
The Well-fed Kitten

Cats are supreme carnivores. Unlike some nominal carnivores, the dog and the wolf, for example, that will eat with omnivorous delight other rations besides meat—and much unlike the panda bear, which is really an herbivore in cuddly disguise—cats adhere rigorously to the notion that flesh is best. This dietary preference is demonstrated in the cat's teeth, which are more suitable for cutting and shearing than they are for grinding, and in the cat's eating behavior, which appears to be designed to avoid plant material no matter how it is presented. Lions, for example, usually do not eat the entrails of their prey, many of which are herbivorous and can be expected, therefore, to have plant material in their gastrointestinal contents. Even when lions have nothing else in their lunch buckets besides entrails, they will empty the entrails first by expressing the contents with their tongues, much as a child pushes the broccoli to one side of the plate. What's more, domestic cats, too, "usually consume the head of their prey first and leave the entrails," say Lon D. Lewis, Mark L. Morris, Jr., and Michael S. Hand, all of whom are doctors of philosophy and veterinary medicine.

This rather large kitten looks as though it will be weaned before long.

Cats do nibble on grass and plants on occasion, especially houseplants of which their owners are fond, but cats cannot extract the carbohydrate nutrients from grass. Thus, greens are medicine-chest, not salad-bar, items for cats, a source of roughage and minerals. Greens also function as an emetic for cats, assisting in the expulsion of hair balls from cats' stomachs by inducing vomiting.

Proteins

If you plan to raise a litter— or if you find out unexpectedly that you are going to be—you should learn the art of bottle feeding, just in case.

Because of their resolute carnivorous habits, cats have developed several unique metabolic needs. The most celebrated is the need for protein (from the Greek *proteios,* meaning *primary*). That need, vis-a-vis the dog's need for protein, becomes more pronounced as a

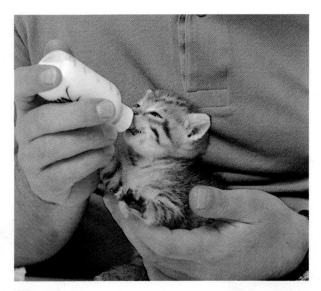

cat grows older. A maturing cat requires half again as much protein as does a growing dog, but an adult cat's protein requirement is twice that of an adult dog's.

Protein, which accounts for more than 50 percent of an animal's dry weight, helps to build and to maintain cells. It provides energy by means of chemical breakdown, inspires muscle contractions, and, dressed up in genes, sends hereditary instructions dancing across generations. Protein is also the stuff of which insulin, digestive enzymes, the antibodies of the immune system, and most hormones are made.

Protein is composed of units of 23 amino acids, which themselves are composed of carbon, hydrogen, oxygen, nitrogen, and sometimes sulfur. Plants synthesize all the amino acids, and, hence, all the protein, they need by combining nitrogen, carbon dioxide, and other chemicals; but the cat, like most other organisms, can manufacture enough of only some amino acids— an even dozen in the cat's case. These are called dispensable amino acids, and they are constructed from other elements such as nitrogen and carbohydrate. The 11 amino acids that a cat cannot synthesize adequately are called essential amino acids. They must be acquired from protein contained in food.

If any of the 11 essential amino acids is lacking in the diet, your pet begins to eat less, to lose weight, and, if it is a kitten, to grow at a slower rate than its littermates do. Other effects of amino-acid deficiency include hyperactivity and spasms, bilateral cataracts, and neurological dysfunction.

Fats

A cat does not live by protein alone. Dietary fat is also an important entree on a cat's menu. Fat is a concentrated energy source, a carrier for fat-soluble vitamins, the wellspring of essential fatty acids, and a carnival for the cat's palate.

Cats easily tolerate and readily use high levels of fat in their diets, but they exhibit, nonetheless, a special need for linolenic and arachidonic acids, neither of which they can convert from linoleic acid, one of the essential fatty acids. Therefore, linolenic and arachidonic acids, which are contained in animal products, must be present in a cat's diet. (Other strict carnivores that cannot convert linoleic acid into linolenic and arachidonic acids are the lion, the mosquito, and the turbot, a carnivorous fish.)

If your pet's diet is deficient in fatty acids, its coat becomes dry and the cat becomes listless. In addition, kittens suffering from fatty-acid deficiency do not grow as quickly as they should, and they are more susceptible to infection.

Carbohydrates

Cats were domesticated originally because they could be trusted to protect grain instead of plundering it. To this day cats in the wild—and cats that earn their keep by protecting feed stored in barns—do

Although it makes for a fetching picture, milk is not an essential—or even a necessary—part of the feline diet after a kitten has been weaned.

not eat grain because they have no need for the carbohydrate it contains. As the National Research Council (NRC) explains, "All animals have a metabolic requirement for glucose [simple sugar] to supply energy for organs, including the central nervous system." Yet even though carbohydrates are an excellent source of sugar, a cat can exist without the sugars and starches contained in carbohydrates as long as it obtains sufficient fat and amino acids in its diet. Grain, nevertheless, chiefly in the form of corn, constitutes a growing portion of the feline diet. This is so because carbohydrates are an economical source of energy and because the cat food industry discovered more than 20 years ago that cats will eat grain as long as it is wrapped in a tasty coating of animal fat. This discovery led to the creation of dry cat food.

Vitamins

Cats cannot reap the benefits from their food without the aid of vitamins, which join forces with protein to create metabolically active enzymes that produce hundreds of important chemical reactions. Vitamins also take part in the formation of hormones, blood cells, nervous-system chemicals, and genetic material.

Four vitamins that cats require—vitamins A, D, E, and K—can be stored in the body's fat reserves. Other essential vitamins—the water-soluble B vitamins, thiamin, riboflavin, pyridoxine, niacin, pantothenic acid, and cobalamin—cannot be stored in the body.

Two of the kitten's vitamin requirements are unique. The first is for preformed vitamin A, which a kitten cannot manufacture by converting beta-carotene. The second is the need for niacin. This results from a kitten's inability to synthesize niacin from tryptophan, an essential amino acid.

Although kittens are more likely to be affected by a lack rather than by an excess of vitamins, a surfeit of vitamins, especially A and D, also can be harmful. Vitamin A toxicity, the consequence of a liver-rich diet, causes skeletal lesions. Vitamin D toxicity, the fallout from injudicious vitamin supplementation, results in calcification of the aorta, the carotid arteries, and the stomach wall.

The most certain way to avoid vitamin toxicity is to refrain from adding vitamins to your cat's food. If the commercial cat food you are feeding is labeled nutritionally complete and balanced, extra vitamins are not going to make it more complete. Adding vitamins to a nutritionally complete and balanced cat food probably will upset the balance of vitamins already in the food and may cause vitamin toxicity. The only cats needing vitamin supplements are those not eating properly because of illness or those losing increased amounts of body fluids because of diarrhea or increased urination.

Minerals

In addition to vitamins, cats need the following nine minerals in order to enjoy optimum health and well-being: calcium, phosphorus, sodium, potassium, magnesium, iron, copper, zinc, and iodine. Cats also are thought to need—primarily because other species need them—manganese, sulfur, cobalt, selenium, molybdenum, fluorine, chromium, silicon, tin, nickel, and vanadium.

Minerals help to maintain tissue structure, fluid balance, and the body's acid-base (electrolyte) balance. Because mineral requirements are interrelated, the same warning about vitamin supplements applies to mineral supplements, too: Proceed with caution and your vet's recommendation, if you proceed at all.

Liquids

Water is the most important nutrient needed to sustain normal cell function. Mammals can lose nearly all their reserves of glycogen and fat, half their protein stores, and 40 percent of their body weight and still survive. The cat, composed of nearly 70 percent water, is in severe metabolic trouble if it loses 10 percent of its body water. Death results if water loss rises to 15 percent. Fortunately, cats can concentrate their urine and conserve water, a strategy that has been passed down to them from their desert-dwelling ancestors.

Food dishes and water bowls should be made of glass, ceramic, or metal.

Water intake is affected primarily by diet. Because canned food is 75 percent water, cats fed canned food exclusively will drink less water than will cats on a combination canned-dry diet or a dry-food-only diet. No matter what kind of food you give your cat, it should have fresh water in a freshly cleaned bowl every day.

As cats mature, they often become deficient in lactase, the enzyme that breaks down lactose in milk. Thus, many adult cats develop diarrhea from drinking milk because they cannot digest it effectively. Nevertheless, cats get along quite well without milk, and there is no need to give milk to kittens once they have been weaned.

from food as completely as a dog's plumbing does. The cat is best served, therefore, by highly digestible foods. A highly digestible food is one from which kittens can absorb at least 85 percent or more of the nutrients available. The best way to insure that your kitten's food is highly digestible is to check the writing on the can or box to see if the food was tested according to Association of American Feed Control Officials (AAFCO) feed-trial protocols. (See How to Decipher a Cat Food Label, page 53.)

Dry, Semimoist, or Canned

Cat food manufacturers invest serious time and money trying to reinvent the mouse. This all-natural, 100 percent nutritionally complete and balanced meal in the soft, gray wrapper supplies the critical mixture of protein, vitamins, minerals, and essential fatty acids a cat requires.

Instead of mice on supermarket shelves, there are close to 100 brands of cat food in three genre: dry, semimoist, and canned. Dry food is less expensive and more convenient to use than canned, and dry food helps to reduce dental tartar to some extent. Canned food is more palatable and, because it is three quarters moisture, is a better source of water than is other food.

No matter what its composition, food passes quickly through the cat's short gastrointestinal tract, which does not wrest the nutrients

Generic, Private Label, Regular, or Superpremium?

Besides having three categories of cat food from which to choose, kitten owners can select generic, private label, regular, or superpremium brands. Generic cat foods, which often do not carry a brand name, usually are produced and marketed locally or regionally, thereby reducing transportation costs and enabling merchants to sell generic foods at cheaper prices. But if generic foods are produced from cheaper materials, they may not provide the nutritional quality of private label, regular, or superpremium foods. Before you buy a generic brand, look for the nutritional claim statement on the label and, just to be safe, buy only those generics whose claims of nutritional adequacy are based on AAFCO feeding-trial procedures. (See How to Decipher a Cat Food Label, page 53.)

Private label foods, which usually bear the house brand name of a grocery store chain, may be manufactured by the same companies that produce generic cat food or they may be manufactured by nationally known companies that also produce their own, more recognizable brands. Instead of the traditional "Manufactured by __," statement that appears on the labels of generic, regular, or superpremium foods, private label brands contain one of the following statements: "Distributed by __," or "Manufactured for __." The same advice offered regarding generic cat food applies to private label brands, too. For greatest security, buy only feed-tested products.

Regular brands are foods with nationwide distribution and nationally recognizable names. There are usually no special nutritional claims made for regular cat foods, beyond, of course, the claims that they are good for your cat and that they meet AAFCO requirements.

Superpremium brands command top dollar and are made with top-of-the-line processing techniques that, manufacturers claim, reduce nutrient loss during heating. Moreover, say manufacturers, superpremium foods are made from higher-quality ingredients: chicken necks or backs instead of chicken by-products such as lung or bone.

All this, manufacturers contend, results in foods with taste, smell, texture, and digestibility that are superior to other kinds of cat food.

Some authorities do not believe, however, that chicken necks are any more nutritious than chicken by-products or that a manufacturer's devotion to aesthetics results in more nutritional miles to the gobble. "Higher-quality ingredients and higher palatability do not make premium foods any better than regular foods," says Quinton R. Rogers, Ph.D., professor of physiological chemistry at the school of veterinary medicine, University of California. "Once you've met the nutritional requirements, you've met them." Thus, a superpremium food with twice as many vitamins as a regular food is not necessarily better than, let alone twice as good as, the regular food. The cat eating the superpremium food, Rogers explains, just loses the excess vitamins in her urine.

Devotees of superpremium foods also claim that their higher digestibility results in lower fecal volume and less fecal odor. The toxicity of fecal odor being in the nose of the beholder, it is impossible to investigate the second of those claims objectively. The lower-fecal-volume claim could be tested, but as one nutritionist has observed, there is little benefit (accrued or otherwise) in scooping up a 2-ounce (60 g) cat dropping vis-a-vis a 1.8-ounce (50 g) pile.

Manufacturers also claim that superpremium food costs no more to feed than does regular food because cats eat less of superpremium than they do of regular food. This claim can be tested easily. If you are feeding your cat one can of food a day and that can costs 48 cents and you are considering switching to a superpremium brand that costs 64 cents a can for the same amount of food, you should be able to feed your cat 48 cents' worth of the superpremium food—or three fourths of a can instead of the whole can you are feeding currently.

To test this theory, weigh your cat on the day you switch to the superpremium brand. Then weigh your pet again a month later. If it has gained more than 2 or 3 ounces (60 to 85 g), cut back on the superpremium food. If it has lost more than 2 or 3 ounces (60–85 g), you will have to increase the amount of superpremium food slightly. Obviously, if your cat has gained weight, the superpremium food costs less to feed than the regular food does; but if your pet has lost weight, the superpremium food costs more.

Consumers also should be aware that superpremium cat foods do not have to meet higher nutritional standards than do regular foods. In fact, says David A. Dzanis, D.V.M., Ph.D., and chairman of the NRC's feline nutrition expert subcommittee, "there is no official definition or clear-cut standards by which to judge superpremium food

as far as the Food and Drug Administration and the AAFCO are concerned. Their role is to insure that products are safe and wholesome. Beyond that, it's a consumer issue, like choosing between chuck steak or filet mignon."

Special Diets

Cats suffering from various diseases often need special diets. For example, cats with hypertension, heart disease, or edema should be on low-sodium diets. Cats with kidney or liver conditions should be fed diets low in protein, phosphorus, and sodium. Cats that are underweight or that suffer from pancreatic or liver disease should be fed highly digestible food. If any of these or other conditions are diagnosed by a veterinarian, he or she may recommend a special diet. Cat owners should follow the veterinarian's instructions faithfully, and, of course, they never should feed a special diet to a cat without first consulting with a vet.

Snacks and Treats

Although no one is a hero to his or her valet, cat owners become instant deities whenever they rattle a box of snacks. No audience is more attentive than cats contemplating a treat.

A considerable subset of the pet food industry is built on this response. Cat owners who become too addicted to the positive reinforcement provided by food-mongering cats are feeding their cats as well as their egos, however. Snacks and treats are nutritionally deficient for full-time use, and your cat is going to want them full time if you offer them too frequently.

You can feed some foods to your cat all of the time, and you can feed all foods to your cat some of the time, but nutritional wisdom is the better part of knowing which time is which. Again, let the label be your guide. If the label says, "Moggy Menu Baked Alaska Bits are intended for intermittent or supplemental use only," then use them intermittently. Do not allow snacks and treats to comprise more than 5 to 10 percent of your cat's diet.

How to Decipher a Cat Food Label

All cat foods have one feature in common: their labels bristle with fine print. Precise editorial guidelines issued by the AAFCO govern the information that must be conveyed on a cat food label. That information must include the product name, the net contents of the package, and the name of the species for which the food inside the package is intended. The manufacturer also must reveal the food's guaranteed analysis, expressed in minimum amounts of crude protein and fat and in maximum amounts of crude moisture and fiber. The name of the manufacturer, packer, or distributor of the food also must appear on the package, but these parties need not disclose a street address if one appears in a current city or telephone directory.

Cat food labels must enumerate, in descending order by weight, any ingredient for which the AAFCO has established a name and a definition. Ingredients not defined by the AAFCO may be called by their common or usual names. The names of all ingredients must be equal in type size, and no ingredient may be listed under a brand or trade name.

If cat food contains artificial colors, they must have tested harmless to cats. Any additives in cat food must conform to federal requirements, be prior sanctioned, or be generally recognized as safe.

While her partners stand guard, the calico cat checks out the food supply.

Cat food labels generally understate the contents of the food they describe. If a manufacturer adds bonemeal, which contains calcium and phosphorous, to a food, the label will say only "bonemeal." Therefore, you will not find all the 40-plus nutrients that cats require listed on a package of food. The nutritionally complete and balanced statement is your clue that those ingredients are present in the food inside the package.

Of all the information to be found on a cat food label, the most important is the nutritional claim made by the manufacturer. Nutritional claims come in two varieties. In the first, the manufacturer declares that Moggy Menu has been shown to provide complete and balanced nutrition in feeding trials conducted according to protocols established by the AAFCO. In the second kind of nutritional claim, the manufacturer attests that Moggy Menu has been formulated to meet the nutrient levels established in the AAFCO's nutrient profiles.

In order to make the feeding trials claim, a manufacturer must compare data obtained from an experimental and a control group of cats, each of which must contain at least eight members. The cats in the experimental group are fed only Moggy Menu for a specified period of time. The control group is fed a diet known to be complete and balanced. At the end of the test period, if the cats that were fed Moggy Menu do not differ significantly along certain variables from the control group, the manufacturer is entitled to claim that Moggy Menu provides complete and balanced nutrition according to the AAFCO's feed trial protocols. The variables on which the experimental and control groups are compared include weight, skin and coat condition, red blood cell count, and other health measures.

In order to make the second kind of nutritional claim—that Moggy Menu was formulated to meet nutrient levels established in the AAFCO nutrient profiles—a manufacturer must sign an affidavit stating that he or she (or they) formulated Moggy Menu from ingredients that will contain, after they have been processed, sufficient levels of all the nutrients the AAFCO has determined a cat food should contain.

The difference between buying a cat food that has been tested in feed trials and one that has been formulated to meet the AAFCO profile is like the difference between buying a preferred stock and a futures option: The consumer can be more confident that the preferred stock (the feed-tested cat food) is going to perform the way it is supposed to perform because it has been fed to real cats in real feeding trials.

The meets-the-nutrient-profiles statement, on the other hand, is somewhat misleading. It does not mean that the AAFCO has analyzed the food in question and has certified that it meets the AAFCO standards. Nor does the statement necessarily mean that the manufacturer tested the food in the can to determine whether it met the AAFCO profiles. This statement simply means the manufacturer formulated the food from ingredients that should have provided enough nutrients to meet the AAFCO profile. We say "should have" because cooking always destroys nutrients in cat food to some extent. Therefore, the nutrients that go into the kettle are always present in greater amounts than the nutrients that finally go into the can.

Individual state regulators are responsible for checking the validity of nutritional claims. If a food is found wanting, the manufacturer is obliged to reformulate that food in order to provide sufficient levels of the nutrients that were lacking.

Some nutritional claims are conspicuous by their absence. Snack foods and treats do not have to contain any statement of nutritional adequacy. What's more, foods intended for intermittent or supplemental use only must be labeled so and should be used only on an intermittent basis.

Thus far only one part of the nutritional claim made on cat food labels has been discussed—the part that tells you the basis on which manufacturers state their claims. There is, however, a second part to nutritional statements—the part that specifies the cats for which the food is intended. Thus, a complete nutritional claim for a feed-tested food will say: "Animal feeding tests using AAFCO procedures substantiate that Moggy Menu provides complete and balanced nutrition for all life stages of the cat." A complete nutritional claim for a meets-the-profile food will say: "Moggy Menu is formulated to meet the nutrient levels established by AAFCO nutrient profiles for all stages of a cat's life." Both these statements assure consumers that they can feed an all-life-stages food to their cats from kittenhood through seniorhood, including motherhood, without worrying.

Instead of being formulated for all stages of a cat's life, some foods are intended for the maintenance of adult cats only, and other foods are intended to support growth and reproduction. The latter are formulated to meet the increased nutritional needs of pregnant females and kittens. These foods must contain more of certain nutrients—more protein, calcium, phosphorus, sodium, and chloride, for example—than do maintenance foods. (Foods providing complete and balanced nutrition for all life stages of a cat also must meet growth and reproduction standards.)

Some critics contend it is impossible for one food to be all things to all life stages of a cat. That argument need not concern nor confuse the new kitten owner. If you are feeding a pregnant female or a kitten, you should choose a growth-and-reproduction or an all-life-stages food. If you are feeding an adult cat, a maintenance food is sufficient and is, perhaps, cheaper than an all-life-stages food.

A Breakthrough in Labeling

One weighty piece of nutritional information that should be present on cat food labels by the time this book is published is the food's caloric content. Previously, the cost of monitoring caloric claims prohibited states from allowing manufacturers to state caloric content. But in 1992 the AAFCO accepted a procedure designed by its feline nutrition expert (FNE) subcommittee that allows states to verify by laboratory analysis the caloric content claims made by manufacturers for their products. In early August 1993 the FNE's recommendation was approved and was passed into regulation.

"Caloric content information is probably more important than the current information on pet food labels," says Dzanis. "Knowing the caloric content will enable consumers to make informed comparisons between products because consumers will have a meaningful way of determining that it is possible to feed X amount of this product and get the same effect as feeding X amount of some other product."

How Much and How Often to Feed

Kittens need relatively more food than adult cats require (see chart).

As the chart indicates, a ten-week-old kitten weighing 2.5

Daily Feeding Guidelines*		Dry	Semimoist	Canned
		(ounces per pound of body weight)		
Kittens:	10 weeks	1.1 oz.	1.4 oz.	3.6 oz.
	20 weeks	.6	.7	1.8
	30 weeks	.45	.6	1.4
	40 weeks	.36	.4	1.2
Adults	Inactive	.32	.4	1.0
	Active	.36	.4	1.2
	Pregnant	.45	.6	1.4
	Lactating	1.00	1.3	3.3

*Adapted from *Nutrient Requirements of Cats*, National Research Council, 1986.

pounds (1.1 kg) would satisfy its daily food requirements by consuming 2.75 ounces (78 g) of dry food or 3.5 ounces (99 g) of semimoist food or 9 ounces (255 g) of canned food a day. A 10-pound (4.5 kg), inactive, adult cat would satisfy its daily food requirements by consuming 3.5 ounces (99 g) of dry food or 4 ounces (115 g) of semimoist food or 12 ounces (340 g) of canned food a day. These amounts may be lower than those specified in the feeding instructions on the cat food package. As food labels underrepresent the contents of the package, they generally overstate the amount of food a cat needs. This generosity on the part of cat food manufacturers is understandable. They would be embarrassed if cats were to lose weight on the recommended feeding amounts. Therefore, they recommend high.

Recommended feeding amounts are estimates based on data collected from many cat feeding trials. A cat's metabolism, influenced by age and activity level, regulates food consumption. One 10-pound (4.5 kg) cat might need half a cup of dry food each day, whereas another might need two thirds of a cup. Pregnant and lactating cats will need more food than other cats.

Though cats prefer their food at room temperature, they are not the notoriously finicky eaters that advertisers paint them to be. Indeed, finicky eaters are made, not born. Two surefire ways to create a finicky cat are by feeding it the same food all the time or by feeding it people food. Give your cat a variety of foods and brands instead: meat and poultry for the most part, with fish for occasional variety. And do not resort to people treats, especially at the table. This is not cute, nor is it necessary for your cat's development.

Because adult cats are so adaptable, their owners have the luxury of choosing among several feeding schedules. Some people feed "wet" food, either canned or homemade, twice a day. Others feed wet food once daily. Some feed wet food once a day and always leave dry food available for their cats. Some people, and many laboratories, feed dry food only.

Kittens wear their pleasures proudly, if not always precisely.

Kittens are not as feeding-flexible as are adult cats. When kittens are being weaned, starting at three to four weeks of age, they should be fed three or four times a day. Reduce feedings to twice a day at six months, and, if you desire, to once a day after a cat's first birthday.

Kittens, by and large, can be fed free choice (i.e., you can leave dry food out at all times) until they are about eight to ten months old. At that point you have to watch to see if you have the cat that can continue to be fed free choice and not put on excessive weight or whether your cat has to be put on a shorter gastro-nomical leash, in which case you put out a measured amount of dry or canned food and when it is gone, it is gone. If you have more than one cat, restricting the diet of one while the others are allowed free choice feeding is much easier said than done.

Switching Diets

Before deciding what to feed your kitten, find out, if possible, what it has been eating. If its diet has been sound, continue with that product or products. Should you need to switch foods, which may happen if you buy a kitten raised on a homemade diet, mix new food with the old in a three-parts-old-to-one-part-new ratio. Every three or four days increase the new food while decreasing the old until the changeover is complete.

Cooking for Your Cat

For many people, feeding their cats is a sacramental experience involving scrupulous adherence to detail. Most home cookers insist that their cats would not be as healthy, sparkling, stress resistant, and economical to feed on a com-mercial diet. They have the eco-nomical part right. Ground meat bought from a pet food provisioner is much less expensive than anything that comes in a box, pouch, or can. But whether raw meat, sometimes cooked and always infused with vitamins, min-erals, oils, and other additives, is better than commercial food is questionable.

Anyone feeding cats a diet based on raw meat must add the right vitamins and minerals in the right proportions. This is more com-plex than pouring calcium, a few tablespoons of vitamins, and some brewer's yeast into the meat and mixing thoroughly. How much cal-cium must you add to raw meat, which is calcium deficient, to restore the calcium-phosphorus ratio to its optimal 1:1 to 1:2 range? How do you convert the 10,000 units of vitamin x per pound listed on the label of a 20-ounce (570 g) jar of cat vitamins into the proper amount that should be added to a pound of raw meat? Which vitamin additive is the most balanced and complete? Does it also contain the proper minerals in the proper amounts and ratios? And should you cook the meat or feed it raw?

Unless you have some special intuition or knowledge that cat food manufacturers with their million-dollar budgets and their battalions of feeding trial cats have overlooked, you should leave the nutritional driving to commercial pet foods. More than nine out of ten cat owners do.

Foods to Avoid

Table scraps: are not nutritionally balanced.

Raw meat: may contain parasites.

Raw fish: may contain parasites and may cause thiamine deficiency.

Raw egg whites: contain a protein that interacts with biotin, rendering it unavailable to the body. Biotin deficiency can cause dried secretions around the eyes, nose, and mouth, as well as scaly skin.

Raw liver: contains an excess of vitamin A.

Bones: may lodge in a cat's throat or pierce the stomach or intestinal wall.

Dog food: does not contain sufficient protein.

Canned tuna for humans: causes vitamin E deficiency.

Chocolate: can diminish the flow of blood and cause heart attacks.

"Yuck! Did you forget to check the expiration date on the carton?"

Chapter 7
Training a New Kitten

If the animal rights movement ever manages to secure voting privileges for pets, cats will flock to the Republican party, for cats are true conservatives. They do not like anything to happen that has not happened before. In fact, cats are creatures of such persistent routine that they do not like the really significant things to happen at different times than they have happened before, with adjustments made for the shift from standard to daylight saving time and back, of course.

Moreover, cats prefer certain resting places, certain toys, and, if they are indulged by their owners, one or two certain foods to the exclusion of all others. This preference for a well-ordered, by-the-numbers existence is somewhat surprising in an animal with a reputation for being a supreme individualist; yet even though cats may not find curiosity altogether killing, they prefer to find it on their own and are largely disconcerted when curiosity finds them instead. Rather than being exasperated by a cat's single-mindedness, however, the crafty owner will turn this inclination to his or her advantage when training a kitten to grow up into a properly conservative, well-behaved cat.

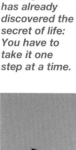

This serious-looking kitten has already discovered the secret of life: You have to take it one step at a time.

How Kittens Learn

Kittens learn by observation, and the first teachers they observe are usually their mothers, who not only know best but who also teach best—if you put any stock in laboratory experiments. In one series of experiments, kittens that watched their mother press a bar to obtain food learned to imitate her behavior faster than did kittens that watched a strange female cat obtain food in the same manner. What's more, kittens that did not have the benefit of any teacher in this situation never figured out that if they pressed the bar they would obtain food. In addition to learning to perform certain behaviors in order to obtain rewards, kittens are also adept at avoiding other behaviors that bring unpleasant consequences (being squirted with a water pistol) and the circumstances (jumping onto the kitchen table) in which those experiences occur.

More interesting than the lessons cats have learned in laboratory experiments is the motivation that inspires cats to learn. Unlike dogs, cats would not produce the desired behavior if their only reward for doing so was a reunion with the experimenter and a couple of pats on the head. Cats expected a more visceral compensation for their performances, and few things are more visceral to a cat than food. The experimenter did wield a modest amount of influence, however. Cats worked more industriously for a reward when that reward was offered by the person who fed them each day.

Kittens exhibited a unique learning characteristic: Among kittens, the freedom to explore was considered a better reward for doing something than was food. This proves that kittens, like people, are not born materialistic. Life, however, in its infinite wisdom, makes them that way.

Like their counterparts in the laboratory, kittens raised in the wild learn best from their mothers; instead of teaching her kittens to hunt, a mother cat creates a learning situation that allows the kittens' instincts to develop naturally. (In sociopolitical gibberish this is called *empowering* the kittens. It is, perhaps, what our cats are trying to do when they lay mice at our doors, although some romantics believe that the mice constitute a present.)

When kittens are roughly five or six weeks old, a mother cat begins to bring dead prey to the nest, where she eats it in front of her kittens. This demonstration stimulates the kittens' natural hunting instincts, and after those instincts have begun to emerge, the mother will bring live (or half live) prey to the nest. After releasing the prey in front of her kittens, the mother intervenes only if the prey appears

Mom is teaching junior how to handle the mail.

to be in danger of escaping. Once the kittens have learned to pounce on their training aids and dispatch them, the mother cat will take the kittens hunting with her.

Because the kittens' hunting lessons depend on a steady supply of visual aids, mothers that hunt best, teach best. Thus, kittens whose mothers are good hunters have a better chance of growing up into good hunters, too; kittens raised by clumsy hunters and kittens that are not raised by a member of their own species at all tend to be lousy hunters; or, in politically correct terms, they are "hunting challenged."

Such is their reliance on observational learning that kittens will imitate their mother's choice of food even if that choice involves foods that a cat ordinarily would not eat. Researchers, to whom such matters seem to be important, have trained adult female cats to eat bananas or mashed potatoes. When those females' kittens were given a choice between meat pellets and either bananas or mashed potatoes, most of the kittens ordered from the fruits-and-vegetables side of the menu.

When to Begin Training

As discussed in chapter two, people acquire kittens in a variety of ways; but whether you searched high and low for just the right kitten or the right kitten searched high and low for you, the best time to begin training that kitten is as soon

Two kittens watching a wide-angle television.

as you have established a rapport with it. Kittens under two months of age have been trained to perform complex visual-pattern discriminations in laboratory settings, and kittens as young as two months of age can be taught to respond to their names at home. Therefore, as soon as your kitten has identified you as the source of food and lavish attention, you should begin teaching the kitten to respond to its name. First, of course, you have to settle on a name.

Selecting a Name

"A good name is better than precious ointment," says Ecclesiastes, 7:1, and a good name is one of a kitten's birthrights. Nevertheless, writes Wayne Bryant Eldridge, D.V.M., in *The Best Pet Name Book Ever* (Barron's Educational Series, 1990), "During my eighteen years as a practicing veterinarian, the majority of recently acquired dogs and cats brought to me for their first examinations have nad no names, not because of apathy on the owner's part but because of the lack of a guide in the name selection process . . . ."

To make up for that lack Dr. Eldridge sorted more than 3,000 pet names into 22 categories, including Appearance, Literature, Art, and Cartoon Characters. Appearance names include Oreo, Blackberry, Fuzzy, and Whiskers. Literary names include Gatsby, Juliet, Tigger, and Tara.

Pairs of kittens, in general, offer possibilities for creative nomenclature that single kittens do not. This is another compelling argument for acquiring more than one kitten. First and Ten, Simon and Schuster, Stanley and Livingston, and Mickey and Minnie are just a few of the harmonious pairs of kitten names that Eldridge presents. Other possibilities include Huntley and Brinkley, Lewis and Clark, Mason and Dixon, and Jagger and Richards; and somewhere in the world there must be (or else there ought to be) a Sturm and Drang, a Rhythm and Blues, a Waylon and Willie; a Sure N' Begorrah, and so forth.

Teaching a Kitten Its Name

Once you have chosen a name for your kitten, you should teach your kitten to respond to that name. The best way to do that is to make the kitten's name synonymous with food. Suppose, for example, you have decided to name your kitten Frasier. Put a few treats in your pocket and have a seat near Frasier one fine morning a few hours after he has been fed or one fine afternoon a few hours before it is time for his dinner. The treat can be a piece of dry or semimoist kibble or some other tidbit in which Frasier has exhibited extreme interest in the past. For best results the treat should be something Frasier does not receive every day as part of his regular diet.

Pronounce Frasier's name clearly and with a jolly, high-pitched, ascending gusto. If he looks in any direction but yours, do nothing. Wait a second or two and say his name again. Unless he is profoundly deaf, Frasier will look toward you eventually. When he does, say "good" and give him a piece of whatever it is you have in your pocket.

You now have Frasier's attention. Pet him a few times and tell him what a good boy he is. Do not, however, say something like "that's a good Frasier" or use his name while praising him. You want him to turn toward you when you say "Frasier," so praise him with generic terms of endearment until he begins to look away from you. As soon as he does, say his name again. You may have to say it once

or twice or even three times, but if you put enough urgency into your tone, Frasier will look at you eventually. When he does, offer him the treat. Praise him a few seconds, and after he is looking elsewhere, say his name again.

After Frasier has responded to his name three or four times in one session, you have accomplished your mission. To build on your initial success, carry those tidbits around the house and break into a spontaneous name-training session several times a day.

Here, Kitty, Kitty

Teaching Frasier to respond to his name leads almost, but not quite, seamlessly into teaching him to come when you call. Once your kitten learns to respond to a vocal summons virtually without fail or serious resistance, you will have established yourself as the nearest thing to a dominant animal in its life, and you will have earned (or bribed your way into) a measure of control over your kitten.

Kittens are not predisposed to answer promptly any summons that does not involve food. Instead of despairing over this tendency, design your first training sessions around it. That is, in fact, what you did when you taught Frasier to respond to his name. Therefore, if he is responding well to his name, teaching him to come when you call should not be difficult.

If you make her name synonymous with food and praise, your kitten will soon learn to respond when you call her.

Many kittens begin loitering in the kitchen well before mealtime. When they see the food bowl descending toward the floor, they zoom toward it instantly. You can make this inclination work to your advantage by saying "Frasier, come," before lowering the bowl from the kitchen counter to the floor. (You could use "here" or any other word instead of "come" when you wish to summon Frasier, but once you have chosen a call word, use it exclusively.)

In addition to rewarding Frasier for coming when you call, be sure to add a lavish helping of praise before you set the bowl down. This will reinforce the behavior you desire because he will associate the word "come" with food and praise.

Some kittens do not appear in the kitchen until they hear the rattle of the dry food container, the sound of a can being opened, or the sound of the drawer where the can opener is kept being opened. If Frasier is one of those kittens, say "Frasier, come" before doing any of these guaranteed-to-get-his-attention activities.

After two or three weeks you will have "trained" Frasier to come where you call, at mealtimes. Perhaps there will be other times of the day and other parts of the house where you will want him to answer this command too. If so, begin this second phase of training (it will be the first phase for those rare kittens that do not race to the kitchen at the sound of the can opener) in a room from which there is no escape and no foolproof place for Frasier to hide. As you did when you trained Frasier to come when you called him to dinner, try to make this lesson fit into his normal routine. If, for example, Frasier likes to sit in the living room window in the afternoon, you might wander into the living room with a few of Frasier's favorite treats in your pocket, close the door quietly, and sit on the sofa. If Frasier begins to come over to greet you, say "Frasier, come" and take a treat out of your pocket. As soon as he is close enough to get the treat, say "good" in a high-pitched, delighted tone and reward him with the treat.

The word "good" serves as a bridging stimulus, that is, a device that teaches a kitten to associate a sound with the arrival of a food reward. Literally, saying "good" is like giving Frasier an IOU at the point at which he did what you wanted him to do. When you say "good," you are saying "Hang on a minute. I'm going to give you something." So after you say "good," the random things a kitten may do while waiting for his reward will not make him confused about what the "correct" behavior was.

Should Frasier appear more interested in what he was doing before you came into the room than in coming over to greet you, move casually to a spot about two or three feet from him. Say "Frasier, come," then offer him the treat. If Frasier comes to you, say "good" and give him the treat. If he ignores you, reach over quietly, pick him up, move him to you, praise him with pats and a hug—but not with the word "good"—and give him the treat. Save "good" for those occasions when Frasier has done what you asked.

Praising a kitten that just has ignored you might not seem like such a bright thing to do, but you would be even less smart to allow Frasier to ignore you when he pleases. By picking Frasier up and moving him to the place where you want him to be, you are teaching him that he is going to come when he is called—one way or another.

If Frasier runs off, do not go running after him at once and do not repeat the "come" command. Walk casually to him instead, pick him up, carry him back to the place from which you first called him, and praise him for coming. Skip the treat this time. You do not want him to think you are a complete pushover. And remember, do not praise him with the word "good" unless Frasier has done the behavior that you asked him to do. "Good" serves only to let him know that what he has just done is a rewardable action.

If Frasier has complied with the "come" command two or three times before refusing, this would be a good time to end the lesson. If he scurries off the first time you call, retrieve him. Praise him for coming, give him a treat, and place him on the floor a foot or two away from

you. Say "Frasier, come" and produce another treat. Unless he is feeling particularly stubborn, he will come for the treat. If he does, say "good" and give him the treat. Then end the lesson. If he is feeling particularly stubborn, pick him up, bring him back to the spot from which you called him, praise him for "obeying," but do not give him a treat. Then end the lesson.

Once Frasier appears to have mastered this command, do not give him a food reward every time he comes when you call. Feline nature being what it is, if he knows he can get a treat every time he comes when he is called, he may decide every so often that it would be more rewarding to continue what he was doing when you called, even if he was doing nothing, than to get that same old predictable treat. But if he does not get a treat every time he comes running or sauntering over when you call, he will begin to think that treats are not always forthcoming. Thus, he will be more likely to answer every time you call because he always will be hoping that this is the time.

Psychologists call this maybe-yes, maybe-no technique intermittent reinforcement. They caution, however, that the intermittent reinforcement must not be predictable itself. If you withhold the treat every third time you summon Frasier, he will soon catch on to that fact and begin timing his refusals to coincide with the empty hand. Intermittent reinforcement must be totally random in order to be totally effective. If your training sessions consist of four or five practices of the "come" command during three or four sessions a day, withhold the treat the second time you call Frasier during the first session, the fourth time during the second session, etc.

Do not be intermittent with your praise, however. You do not want Frasier thinking you take him for granted. Nor do you want him to think that you love him any the less for some performances than for others. Every time he comes when you call, say "good," even if you do not give him a treat.

Repeat the "come" exercise a few times a day. At first keep the distance between Frasier and you to three or four feet and limit each session to two or three minutes in which Frasier has answered your call three or four times. After Frasier is coming to you consistently when you call, increase the distance between you and him by gradual increments: first, to four or five feet for several days and then, to six or seven feet for several days. Keep increasing the distance between you and him until he responds to your command from across the room.

If you want to impress yourself, try calling Frasier from the next room. For obvious reasons, the kitchen is the best room for you to be in when you first attempt this feat, and the best thing to do right after you call him is to rattle a box of dry food. After he is bounding regularly into the kitchen in

response to this stimulus, call him without shaking the box, and give him plentiful applause and a treat if he comes running. If he does not, call him again and rattle the box this time. When Frasier appears, praise him and give him a treat.

Once Frasier is racing to the kitchen in response to your voice alone, try calling him while you are in other rooms in the house. If Frasier is an only child, use the dry food box as an training aid at first, then try calling him by voice only. If you have other cats, the sound of the dry food box might draw a crowd, so you might not be able to use this technique unless you can confine them to another room first.

If at any point Frasier does not respond to your vocal summons from another room, do not make an issue of it and do not repeat the command. Perhaps he did not hear you, and even if he did, the worst conclusion he will reach is that he can ignore you on occasion when you are not in the same room as he. Even in that event you will still be miles ahead of the game. Most cats figure they can ignore their owners from any distance at any time.

Unless you have visions of retiring on the money Frasier earns in the movies—or unless you have a fenced in, escape-proof yard—you need not practice the "come" command anywhere but in the house. Some cat trainers suggest taking Frasier to a friend's house for a practice session, but asking a friend if you and Frasier can drop by to work on obedience training is somewhat forward. (There is nothing wrong, however, with asking a friend to come over for a visit and then having Frasier stroll by for a show-and-tell at the same time.)

After you are satisfied with Frasier's response to the "come" command, test his resolve, and yours, by adding some distractions to the routine. Call him while he is sitting in the living room window watching traffic. Call him when he is playing with a toy or with another cat. If he responds, good for him and you. If he does not, you will have to pick him up, carry him to the spot from which you summoned him, and reward him with praise and a treat.

From Frasier's point of view, there are few reasons for calling a cat who lives indoors, and all of those reasons involve food. Whenever you call Frasier, he should be happy you did. Never call him when

"There's one in every family. As soon as you get comfortable, she bursts in with a camera."

you want to give him medication, stuff him into a carrier for a trip to the vet's, or do anything else that might cause him discomfort. If he associates a summons with an unpleasant consequence, he will begin ignoring all summonses.

Litter Pan Training

According to conventional wisdom, kittens are taught to use a litter pan by their mothers, but some animal behaviorists dispute that wisdom. As proof, they point to evidence, both scientific and anecdotal, of orphaned kittens using a litter box without ever being shown how to do so by an adult cat.

When kittens begin walking at about four weeks of age, they instinctively begin scratching and playing in soft, loose surfaces. As they mature, in addition to playing in loose surfaces they begin to eliminate in them, and they will do that without ever having seen an adult animal doing it.

Behaviorists also challenge the notion that the best way to teach an orphaned or a recalcitrant kitten to use a pan is by placing it in the pan, taking its front paws in your hands, and making scratching motions with the kitten's paws in the litter. That technique may do more harm than good. You could create litter box problems by doing it because the kitten might not like being handled that way and might begin to avoid the pan as a result.

No matter how your kitten learns to use a pan, there are several elementary principles of litter pan training with which you should be familiar. Always keep the pan in the same quiet, easy-to-reach place. While your new kitten is getting used to its novel surroundings, place it gently into the pan after meals, naps, and spirited play to reinforce its instincts. Praise your kitten quietly after it has used the pan. Do not allow your pet to wander far from the litter-pan room unless you are along to supervise. If you leave your kitten home alone, confine your pet to the room in which the litter pan is located.

Dirty pans often can be the cause of accidents. All waste should be scooped out of the pan and disposed of each day. Additional litter should be added to the pan as required. Once a week—or sooner if your nose suggests—dump all the litter, wash the pan thoroughly with a mild, nonammonia-based cleaner, rinse well, and put 1 to 2 inches (2.5–5 cm) of fresh litter into the pan.

If your kitten is comfortable with one kind of litter, stick with that brand. Kittens are creatures of habit as well as cleanliness. Switching litter may upset your kitten's routine, which might result in accidents. If you must, for some reason, train your kitten to use a new litter, add a small, unnoticeable amount of the new litter into the old kind at the weekly litter change. Every week add increasing amounts of the new litter to the mix until the changeover has been effected.

Scratching Post Training

Kittens scratch for two reasons: to remove the dead, outer husks from their claws and to mark territory, both visually and with scent from glands in their paws. Whatever their motivation, kittens are without consciences regarding the surfaces into which they sink their claws. They will scratch wherever and whenever it feels good, and kitten owners must concentrate their kittens' scratching behavior on surfaces that kitten and owner find mutually acceptable. Most owners prefer that those surfaces be wrapped around a scratching post.

Two members of the notorious James Gang holed up in their mountain retreat.

A scratching post is better than Scotch Guard for protecting furniture, but scratching posts should be installed in your house before you install your kitten, thereby enabling you to show your kitten where the post is—and what it is for—after you have shown your pet to the litter pan. (Like litter pans, scratching posts should be deployed—at least one to a story—on every story of the house to which your kitten has access.)

Kitten owners can lessen the amount of husk-removal scratching their kittens engage in by seeing that the kittens' claws are clipped regularly. (See Clipping Your Kitten's Claws, page 79.) Clipping removes the tip of the claw and, in the bargain, the husk of dead claw, if there is one, that covers the fresh claw underneath. If their claws are clipped once a week or so, kittens will have less need to remove the husks of dead claws by scratching—an activity frequently mistaken for sharpening the claws.

No matter how attentive you are to Ruffles's claws, she will still want a good scratch now and again if for no other reason than because it feels so good to stretch her muscles in the process. Fortunately, this need not be prevented. Redirecting her attention to a scratching post will mollify you and Ruffles both.

To teach Ruffles to use a scratching post, wave a toy directly in front of it so that Ruffles's nails dig into the post when she grabs for the toy. Two or three times after realizing how good it feels to sink her claws into the post and yank them out, she will begin to think of the scratching post as a home-amusement center. Then wave the toy farther up the post so that she is encouraged to climb up after the toy. Play this game two or three times a day for a few days and soon Ruffles will be climbing the post on her own.

Because kittens have scent glands in their paws, scratching leaves a kitten's signature on whatever she scratches. This phenomenon works to an owner's benefit with scratching posts. The more a post reminds a kitten of herself, the more she will be inclined to return there, kittens being more than a little narcissistic.

Kittens also scratch to mark territory, and this kind of scratching most often occurs near places where kittens sleep, near entrances to rooms, or in areas where kittens see or encounter other cats. If you allow Ruffles to sleep on your $2,000 Corinthian-leather sofa, you should not blame her if she rips a few divots out of the sofa when she wakes up—no matter how closely you have stationed a scratching post.

If that sofa is near a window through which Ruffles can see the next door neighbor's cat using your lawn for a latrine, Ruffles is liable to scratch the sofa by way of showing the offending cat whose lawn that is and warning her to take her business elsewhere. If such is the case, you could move the sofa, board up the window, lock up your neighbor's cat, or deny Ruffles access to the living room, library, or den in which your slowly disintegrating sofa is located.

Wherever Ruffles is doing her delinquent scratching, you should inspect the scene of the crime carefully. Is there a scratching post in the area where the delinquent scratching is perpetrated? What about the object Ruffles is using instead of her post? Is it more coarse than the scratching post? Or is it more soft and yielding? Is the forbidden object horizontal or vertical?

If there is no post in the crime scene area, put one there—as close as possible to the violated surface—and teach Ruffles how to use the post. If there is a post nearby already, perhaps you should remove its surface covering and replace it with a material more closely resembling the rug or sofa on which Ruffles has been scratching instead. Or perhaps you should not replace the covering at all if Ruffles has been working out on a table leg. If the unwanted scratch marks indicate that Ruffles prefers a low-slung or a floor-mounted scratching surface (some kittens crouch when they scratch) install a suitably configured, horizontal scratching post in that area.

In addition to giving Ruffles a safe scratching alternative to the surface on which she has been scratching illicitly, you should make the forbidden surface as unappeal-

ing as possible by covering it with double-sided sticky tape, aluminum foil, a sheet of sandpaper, or a plastic carpet runner, pointy side up. You might also attach cotton balls soaked in muscle rub ointment or some other unpleasant smelling medium to the surface you want her to avoid.

Keep the new post as close to the former crime scene as possible, and keep the scratching deterrents on the forbidden objects until Ruffles uses the new scratching post without fail for two weeks. Then remove the coverings or scents from the forbidden surface gradually.

If a scratching post next to the living room sofa offends your decorator's sensibilities, once Ruffles has returned to the straight and narrow—or to the horizontal and wide—gradually move the post, a

Most kittens enjoy a good scratch upon waking. Keep this in mind if you allow your kitten to sleep on the sofa.

foot or so at a time, to a location in the room that you and your decorator find more acceptable.

No Chewing or Begging Allowed

If you discover your kitten nibbling on the leaves of a plant in the living room, you are served better by creating a negative experience for the kitten—by squirting it with a water pistol, for example—than by removing your pet from the plant site and saying no. If you squirt Terminator with a water pistol—provided, of course, you do not announce yourself as the squirter by shouting at him before you do—he will associate the plant with the negative experience of getting wet. If he makes enough associations like that, eventually he will leave the plant alone.

The squirt gun technique is limited in its application. For it to be effective, you have to stake out the plant in the living room and wait patiently, gun in hand, every time Terminator is visiting there. Eternal vigilance may be the price of freedom, but a well-behaved kitten need not be such a costly proposition. Better to create another negative experience for which the plant will get the blame. To do this, apply Bitter Apple, Sour Grapes, Tabasco sauce, or any other nasty tasting but nontoxic substance to the leaves of the plant. This dash of prevention is worth more than a squirt of cure.

Relying on punishment alone to resolve a behavior problem after it has occurred is generally less effective than using a negative experience to prevent the behavior from happening. Besides, if Terminator has developed a strong attraction to a certain plant, he might risk a soaking to nibble on its leaves occasionally; and if you are not there to administer the soaking, he will keep on nibbling. But if the plant leaves a bad taste in his mouth every time he starts snacking on it, he soon will leave the plant alone.

Some people do not approve of using a squirt gun or a foul-tasting substance to persuade a kitten to refrain from an unwanted behavior. If these methods make you uneasy, you could close the doors to the rooms where Terminator menaces your plants, you could keep only hanging plants in your house, or you could grow some greens for

Cats believe in stopping to smell the flowers, then eating them.

Terminator to chew on and show him to those greens every time you find him nibbling on forbidden fronds. In fact, you should provide homegrown treats for Terminator to chew on no matter what method you use to keep him away from your plants.

Taste-aversion therapy also puts the bite on other forms of unwanted chewing around the house. If your kitten develops a taste for the corners of the sofa cushions or the bedspread, season them with Bitter Apple or Tabasco. Do the same to the corners of books or magazines, your slippers, bathroom towels, and any other objects you do not want your kitten to chew.

Some professional cat trainers have advised cat owners to smear Tabasco sauce on their cats' gums to show the cats how unpleasant it tastes at the same time they (the owners) smear Tabasco on various objects the cat is not supposed to chew. What's more, cat owners have been advised to take an object that a cat has chewed and ruined, spread Tabasco sauce on it "really heavily," and stuff the object into the cat's mouth. This advice, in addition to bordering on the malicious, violates one of the principles of cat training because it constitutes punishment after the fact. A cat whose sensitive mouth tissues have just been torched is not going to make the necessary connections between the chewing he did and the cruel and unusual punishment he received. Besides, if the object is already ruined, it is beyond saving, and so is any cat owner who would be senseless enough to follow this advice. If there is anything priceless and irreplaceable in your house that could be destroyed if your kitten chews it, make sure that object is beyond your kitten's reach.

Begging is the easiest trick for a kitten to learn and the most difficult trick to unlearn. Once Terminator has been rewarded for soliciting a bite of your Peking crispy duck, you will have created a furry little monster. Expect to find this monster hovering about at mealtimes, a resolute mendicant, all eyes and appetite.

If you do not want Terminator nosing around your plate or potato chip bag, you must discourage him each and every time he does, without fail. What is done is not easily

A cat is seldom more appealing— or more human-esque—than when it is standing on two feet. (And we are more catlike when we are on all fours.)

undone once you begin feeding a kitten out of your hand.

On the other hand, kittens can be taught not to beg. To stop that kind of behavior, put the flat of your hand on the kitten's forehead, push gently but firmly, and make a hissing sound. That is a natural way of telling the kitten to buzz off. Indeed, that is how the kitten's mother would talk to him.

Because kittens are inclined to interpret any push, no matter how slight, as an aggressive action, you need not be overenthusiastic in delivering this message. You do not want to scare the kitten. You just want to appeal to his natural instinct to back down to a more dominant cat.

A kitten hanging 18 on the drapery.

Thou Shalt Not Jump

You are sitting at the kitchen table one morning with only your favorite section of the newspaper between you and the day's burdens. You are about to sink a fork into your eggs Benedict when Terminator jumps onto the table to investigate. With the swiftness of a karate master, you rap your fork sharply against your plate. If you are using the best china that morning, you could substitute a 20-megaton foot stomp. No matter what its source, if the sound you make is startling enough, Terminator should beat feet immediately to lower ground.

You could probably achieve the same response by rattling the newspaper, smacking the underside of the table with your fist, or making any abrupt, unsettling noise. If you happen to be wearing a whistle that morning, an extended blast or two will work nicely.

Do not swat at Terminator with your hand, leap up waving your arms like a dictator, or make any other sudden, aggressive motion toward him. If you strike him accidentally, you may make him hand shy. If you rise up menacingly from the table, bellowing like an enraged water buffalo and snorting fire, he will certainly leap off the table and race out of the room, but he also may begin racing out of the room any time he is in the kitchen and sees you getting up from the table.

Although kittens are sensitive enough to cease and desist when they are startled, they are curious enough to return to the scene of a misdemeanor. Do not be discouraged, therefore, if Terminator lands in the middle of the breakfast table the morning after he was startled off by the clang of a fork on china or the stomp of your foot on the floor. Be prepared to repeat whatever measure it was that ran him off the first day, and be prepared to escalate the war of wills—even if it means coming to the breakfast table armed with a squirt gun or a whistle each morning.

It should go without saying, which is probably why it needs to be said, that there is a difference between creativity and cruelty in training a kitten. If, when your kitten jumped onto the breakfast table, you grabbed him by the scruff of the neck and dunked his nose into a steaming cup of coffee, he probably would refrain from jumping onto the table again. He also might burn his nose. He surely would lose faith in you, and he most likely would be unwilling to come when you called or to show you the kind of affection it is the kitten's special province to bestow.

Getting Terminator off the table once he already has beamed himself up is quickly accomplished. Getting him to refrain from jumping on the table altogether takes better timing. To accomplish this, the well-trained owner anticipates the kitten's arrival, sees him skulking around the table, and makes a loud noise or barks "no" as soon as the kitten goes into a preleap crouch.

Though you make enough noise to startle your kitten, you should keep your corrections impersonal. That is best achieved by not taking your kitten's actions personally. He did not jump onto the table to get your dander up. So keep your dander down. All he wanted was to find out what was going on up there, and all you want is a kitten-free kitchen table.

The best time to determine what you want from your kitten is before he starts doing what you do not want. Therefore, you should decide what places are going to be off-limits before you bring your kitten home.

"That's just like you. I take your queen and you sit on the board."

The Mischief-proof Environment

Because it is easier to modify a kitten's environment in many cases than it is to modify its behavior, the best way to keep kittens out of mischief is to keep mischief out of kittens' reach. The well-behaved kitten is most often the kitten with the fewest opportunities to misbehave. Thus, if there are rooms in the house you do not want your kitten to explore, keep the doors to hose rooms closed. If there are fragile objects in the rooms your kitten is allowed to visit, put them out of climbing range. (See Kitten-proofing Your House, page 36.)

The privilege of keeping kittens—and it is a privilege, not a right—is accompanied by the responsibility of keeping them healthy and content. If you do not want Terminator climbing the drapes, you must provide him with something he can climb. If you do not want Terminator scratching the sofa, you must provide him with something into which he can sink his claws. If you do not want Terminator eating the houseplants, you must provide him with homegrown grasses for nibbling. In short, you must be creative enough to find ways of recapitulating a kitten's natural world in an artificial indoor environment—providing toys that inspire hunting and chasing, cat "trees" that extend an opportunity to climb, secluded areas that furnish privacy, and windows that afford an opportunity to observe the world from which indoor kittens are excluded. In addition, catnip for the occasional high and comfortable beds for sleeping should all be part of the indoor kitten's environment.

Cats interpret any loose string as an invitation to go fishing.

Chapter 8
Kitten Care and Grooming

Grooming is the art of removing dead hair from a kitten so that it does not have to remove it itself. Although kittens inherit a deserved reputation for cleanliness and personal hygiene, all kittens need some help with grooming; and nature has produced some varieties—namely, Persians and other longhair kittens—with profuse coats that are thick enough and long enough to warrant more than casual attention. What's more, virtually all cats, regardless of coat length, do shed. Regular grooming removes dead hair from a cat's coat and eliminates the necessity of removing that hair from the furniture, the rugs, or your clothing—or from the bottom of your foot after you have encountered a foul, oozing hair ball while you are making your way to the kitchen for a snack at 1 A.M.

Shorthair kittens do not have to be groomed as frequently as longhair kittens do. One or two grooming sessions a week will keep your shorthair kitten looking spiffy. Nor do shorthair kittens require much bathing, especially if they never go outdoors. Indeed, absent a plague of fleas in your house—in which case flea baths are in order—shorthair kittens can live quite happily without ever being bathed, and you will live quite happily for not having to bathe them.

Longhair kittens, however, need grooming three times a week on the average, and because the hair on their hindquarters can get soiled when they use the litter pan, they will need a bath more frequently than a shorthair kitten will.

If you got your kitten from a breeder, it should not be shy around

Kittens love to get together and to stare into space or at their well-groomed navels.

then groom the kitten there the next. If there are no tables in your house on which the kitten is allowed to nap or to explore, perhaps you should consider visiting a pet shop or a cat show to price grooming tables.

The Right Tools

Do not show up at the grooming table unless you have set out the tools that will be required for the job. You will need all of the following tools some of the time and some of the following tools all the time. Your goal for a particular grooming session—a routine, lick-and-a-promise maintenance or a close-attention-to-details makeover—will determine which of the following tools you will need:

- Comb(s) or brush(es)
- Cotton swabs
- Face cloth
- Nail clippers
- Lukewarm water
- Mineral oil
- Paper cup or other receptacle for dead hair

If you have a shorthair kitten, you need only two combs to keep that kitten looking stylish: a flea comb and a grooming comb with teeth about ⅝ inch (1.6 cm) long and 1/16 inch (0.2 cm) apart. In some combs the tight, flea-catching teeth occupy half the comb's length while the all-purpose teeth occupy the other half. If you would feel more comfortable

Handsome is as handsome is groomed.

a comb or a brush. If you found your kitten—or it found you—in some other fashion, it may not be as happy about being groomed at first. If so, you should introduce your kitten to a comb and/or brush as soon as your pet is settled in its new surroundings. Keep the grooming sessions brief at first: five to ten minutes every second or third day until the kitten is used to being handled.

If you do not have a proper grooming table—and unless you are a professional groomer or a cat breeder, chances are you do not—you can groom your kitten on a table or a counter in the kitchen or the bathroom. Do not groom your kitten on any surface, the kitchen table, for example, that is otherwise off limits to the kitten. If you chase your kitten from the table one day

by adding a third comb to your arsenal, choose one whose teeth are closer together than $\frac{1}{16}$ inch (0.2 cm). No matter what size or style of comb you choose, make sure that the teeth on the comb are rounded. Pointy teeth can cause your kitten pain. If you are not sure whether the teeth are too pointy or not, run the comb lightly across your forearm. If that hurts, get another comb.

A good all-around comb for grooming a longhair kitten has teeth that are $\frac{7}{8}$ inch (2.2 cm) long and are divided into two sections of equal length. The teeth on one half of the comb are almost $\frac{3}{16}$ inch (0.5 cm) apart. The teeth on the other half are a little more than $\frac{1}{16}$ inch (0.2 cm) apart. If you want to buy a good second comb for longhairs, choose one that has teeth about $\frac{5}{8}$ inch (1.6 cm) long and a little less than $\frac{1}{16}$ inch (0.2 cm) apart.

Some people like combs with teeth of alternating length, $\frac{7}{8}$ inch (2.2 cm) and $\frac{3}{4}$ inch (1.9 cm), for grooming longhairs. Other kitten owners recommend combs with $\frac{5}{8}$ inch (1.6 cm) long teeth that rotate as they move through the kitten's coat. The rotating action of the teeth helps to remove dead hair from the kitten without tugging too roughly on the kitten's skin.

Like combs, grooming brushes are manufactured in different materials and shapes, and brushes also have bristles made of various kinds of materials: animal hair, plastic, or stainless steel. The tips of stainless steel brushes are often covered with tiny, plastic balls that protect a kitten's skin from puncture wounds. Some brushes are two-sided: sporting natural bristles on one side and stainless steel or synthetic bristles on the other. The nylon- or plastic-bristle brushes, many people report, can damage a kitten's coat and generate static electricity, which makes grooming difficult and turns a longhair coat into a fright wig. The same warning regarding the teeth on a comb applies to the bristles on a brush: the tips of the bristles should not be so sharp as to inflict pain on your kitten.

Clipping Your Kitten's Claws

Because you may encounter your kitten's claws unexpectedly while you are grooming your kitten,

Having their claws clipped is an acquired taste for cats. The earlier they acquire that taste, the better.

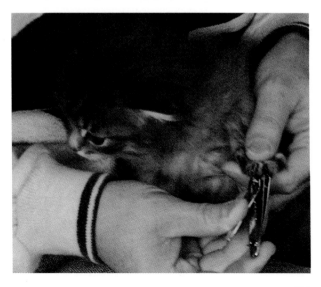

begin each grooming session by checking them. Place your kitten on a table, facing away from you, or on your lap, facing away from you. Lift one of the kitten's legs so that the lower part of the leg is held in your upturned fingers. Hold the leg securely between the heel of your thumb and the tips of your middle, ring, and little fingers, but do not exert undue pressure on the leg. With the kitten's leg thus secured, grasp the kitten's foot between your thumb and forefinger. Press the kitten's foot with your thumb, spreading the kitten's toes and extending its claws. Inspect each claw individually. The claw does not need cutting if the end is blunt or rounded. If the nail ends in a needlelike point, it does need clipping. Be careful to clip only the hooked part of the claw. Do not cut into the visible, pink vein, which is called the quick, inside the nail.

A lap is a serviceable, organic grooming table.

Combing or Brushing a Kitten

Many kittens are ticklish—and hence less amenable to grooming on their bellies, hindquarters, or other areas. Therefore, do not begin by attacking one of these sensitive zones. Instead, begin by grooming an area such as the back of the neck or the base of the spine that is more likely to elicit purrs from your kitten.

The Comb-through Method

Begin combing or brushing with the lie of the coat. (The lie is the direction in which the coat points.) Glide the comb into the coat gently at about a 45° angle. Do not exert great pressure or lean down constantly on the comb. Instead, move the comb carefully and smoothly across the kitten's body. Keep your wrist locked so you do not take any divots out of your kitten's skin. This approach works just as well if you are using a brush instead of a comb, the only difference being that the bristles of a brush will enter the coat at a 90° angle.

Many young kittens will try to avoid a grooming session. Thus, you may need to wield the comb or brush with one hand while you steady the kitten with the other hand. For example, you may need to place your free hand on the kitten's chest while you comb its back and sides; or you may place your free hand, palm up, on the kitten's

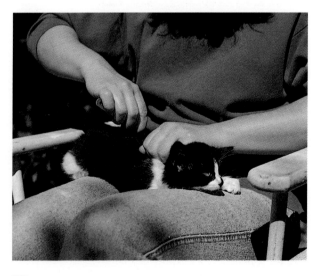

underbelly while you comb its hindquarters or neck.

Although kittens can be ticklish on their underbellies, you can comb a kitten there by placing the kitten on the table facing away from you and then lifting your pet's front legs with one hand while you comb with your other hand. This works best if you place your free hand, palm up, just behind and above the midpoint of the kitten's front legs. Lift the kitten's legs gently until the kitten is standing on its hind legs with its back at about a 60° angle to the table. (If the kitten is facing you, place your free hand palm down instead of palm up when you lift the kitten's front legs off the table.)

Kittens should be combed twice during each grooming session: once to look for flea dirt, skin rashes, or mats in the coat, particularly in the "armpits" of the kitten's front legs, and once to get out the dead hair you missed the first time through. If you find flea dirt, you should give your kitten a flea bath or try to eliminate the fleas with a powder or mousse that is safe to use on kittens. If you kitten has a rash, schedule an appointment with the veterinarian, who can assess the problem and prescribe treatment.

If you encounter a small mat about the size of a marble in your kitten's coat, do not try to rake the mat out with the comb or brush. Take the mat in both hands, instead, holding the right half between the thumb and forefinger of your right hand and the left half between the thumb and forefinger of your left hand. Pull tenderly in opposite directions, being careful to pull parallel with your kitten's skin. The mat should separate into two, smaller mats. Repeat the procedure, separating the two mats into four. The mats may then be small enough and loose enough to be tugged out carefully, one at a time, with the comb. If they are not, separate them once more and then comb them out.

Do not try to remove an overly large mat with the method just described. Make an appointment with a professional groomer or a veterinarian and have the mat shaved off.

If you are determined to remove the mat yourself, first cut it with scissors, leaving about 0.5 inch (1.3 cm) of mat. Do not try to cut the mat any closer to the skin or you might cut the kitten instead. You may then be able to subdivide the mat into small sections that can be teased out with a comb.

The Lift-and-Flip Technique

After you have combed or brushed your kitten once, repeat the procedure; but this time, instead of combing in long strokes, use shorter strokes that lift and flip the kitten's hair, thereby aerating the coat and producing a soft, radiant look. Start at the base of the kitten's tail, and slide the comb or brush gently into the kitten's coat, stopping just as you reach the skin.

Then, lift the hair against its natural lie by flicking your wrist lightly in an upward, counterclockwise motion. Continue this backcombing process until you have made your way to the kitten's head. Then run the comb or brush as your normally would through the just combed portion of the kitten to return the coat to its natural lie. You can backcomb the kitten's sides in the same fashion, working from the spine to the ends of the ribs. (Backcombing works on long hair and short hair kittens alike.)

To backcomb a short-haired kitten's underbelly, lift its front legs off the table as you did before, but before you do make sure the kitten is facing the same direction that you are. Instead of combing with the lie of the coat, you are going to begin combing just in front of the hind legs and then work delicately toward the front legs. You can skip the lift-and-flip approach here. Regular strokes will do just fine as you comb the hair toward the kitten's front legs as you go.

A long-haired kitten's underbelly can be backcombed front to back or back to front. If you use the latter method, face the kitten when you lift its front legs. Begin combing right in front of your kitten's hind legs. Instead of flicking your wrist counterclockwise (away from you) as you did when backcombing the kitten's back and sides, flick your wrist clockwise (toward you). Repeat this stroke, moving the comb or brush an inch or so toward

you each time until you reach the kitten's front legs.

A kitten's legs are combed or brushed downward with short strokes. For a finished appearance, you can comb or brush the legs upward to give them a fuller look.

To groom the short hair kitten's tail, cup it on the underside with one hand about midway along the tail. Comb softly with the lie of the coat, moving the comb in 2- or 3-inch (5–7.6 cm) increments from the tip to the base of the tail.

As has been noted, many long hair kittens are sensitive about their armpits. These areas should be combed, therefore, with great care. Lift your kitten's leg and comb gently downward until the hair has been separated. Comb once more, this time in the opposite direction, if your kitten will tolerate the extra attention.

To groom the long hair kitten's tail, hold it gingerly by its tip. Move the comb or brush through the tail and toward you in short, incremental strokes, working from the tip to the base of the tail. Then comb the tail again, but this time use the lift-and-flip technique, flicking your wrist clockwise (toward you) as you work your way down the kitten's tail from tip to base.

Do not be surprised if your kitten jumps off the table while you are grooming. Simply retrieve the kitten and return it to the table—even if you had just about had enough of grooming when the kitten decided that it did. (To make retrieving the kitten easier, close the doors to the room before you begin grooming.) Continue grooming for a while—at least for another minute or so—even if you were nearly finished grooming when your kitten tried to make its escape. Continuing the grooming session as if nothing happened lets your kitten know that grooming is finished when you say so, not when it does.

Bathing Your Kitten

The most comfortable setting in which to bathe a kitten is the kitchen sink. A sink of a comfortable size is at least 19 inches (48 cm) wide, 16 inches (41 cm) long, and 6.5 inches (17 cm) deep. If your sink does not have a built-in spray attachment, you can buy one at a hardware store. You will probably also need an adapter that will enable you to hook the sprayer to the faucet on your sink.

Bathing a kitten can go a lot easier and a good deal more quickly if you talk a spouse or other family member into lending a hand. You would also be wise to have a cat carrier ready with an absorbent towel covering the floor of the carrier, in case your kitten goes ballistic during the bath and needs to dry out before being released.

You should not show up at the sink before you have set out the implements you will need for bathing your kitten. These include:
- Comb(s) or brush(es) or both
- Two terrycloth washcloths

Cats are incapable of being wet and looking happy at the same time.

- Regular or flea shampoo
- Three bath towels
- Cotton balls
- Eight stacks of prefolded paper towels, about six panels thick
- Blunt-tipped scissors
- Toothbrush
- Two small bowls of lukewarm water
- Mineral oil in a squeeze bottle
- Mechanic's-hand-soap solution (optional)
- Hair dryer (optional)

After gathering the requisite materials and summoning up your resolve, cover the bottom of the sink with a rubber mat or a bath towel. This will provide secure footing—and perhaps a feeling of security—for your kitten. Cats that start to slip often start to flail their feet, with their claws out.

Before putting your kitten into the sink, check the kitten's claws. If they need clipping, clip them.

Then check your kitten's ears. Remove visible dirt with a cotton swab or a cotton ball moistened with hydrogen peroxide or mineral oil. Then put a small wad of cotton into each ear to prevent water from finding its way into the ear canal and possibly causing infection. Put a few drops of mineral oil into each of the kitten's eyes to protect them from stray shampoo.

If your kitten's face needs washing, clean it with lukewarm water and a face cloth. Faces that are more than a little dirty can be cleaned with a weak solution of water and tearless shampoo. Squirt a few drops of shampoo into a bowl of lukewarm water, stir, and, using a washcloth, rub the solution carefully into the soiled areas on your kitten's face. Rinse by dipping a clean washcloth into a clean bowl of lukewarm water and rubbing the shampoo out of the fur.

It is important to do all of this auxiliary grooming before you put your kitten into the sink. The opportunity for mishap grows in proportion to the amount of time a cat is immersed in water. It is also important to remove all rings and jewelry before you bathe your kitten. If the kitten decides to bolt in midbath, you do not want one of its claws snagged for better or for worse in a ring, bracelet, or necklace.

When at last you are ready to put your kitten into the sink, turn on the water and adjust the temperature, testing with your wrist to make sure that the water is not too hot. If the water feels uncomfortably warm to you, chances are it will feel the same way to your kitten. Adjust the temperature accordingly. Make sure, too, that the house temperature is at least 72°F (22°C).

When the moment of immersion is at hand, place your kitten into the sink and let the water and the good times roll. If your kitten has a greasy tail, or if the kitten's coat is greasy in any spots, take a handful of the mechanic's-hand-soap solution, rub it into the greasy site, and work the solution into the coat. (To prepare the degreasing solution, combine half a can of hand soap, which is available at hardware stores, with an equal amount of water and let the mixture stand over night.)

After massaging the hand-soap solution into the greasy area(s), rinse the soap until it is out of your kitten's coat completely. You are finished rinsing when the water coming off the kitten is as clear as the water going onto it.

After you have degreased any offending spots on your kitten, wet it down thoroughly with the spray attachment until the kitten is soaked to the skin. If you are using flea shampoo on your kitten, wet its neck thoroughly at once and lather the kitten's neck well to prevent fleas on the kitten's body from escaping to its face. Then proceed to lather the rest of the kitten. (When using a flea shampoo, check the label first to see if the shampoo is safe for use on kittens and if the manufacturer recommends leaving the shampoo on the coat for a while before rinsing.)

If you are not using a flea shampoo, apply the regular shampoo, lathering the coat generously, as soon as you have wet your kitten with the spray attachment. Never lather past the kitten's neck because you might get shampoo into its eyes. To clean behind the kitten's ears, put some shampoo on the toothbrush and brush the shampoo into the hair directly behind the ears.

After your kitten has been lathered profusely, begin rinsing.

There are three secrets to a clean coat: rinse, rinse, and rinse. Some people use a premixed vinegar-and-water solution as a final rinse for optimum soap-scum removal. About half a cup of vinegar in a gallon of water is sufficient. Other people prefer a conditioning rinse manufactured for human use.

After your kitten has been rinsed, take hold of its tail at the base with one hand, as if you were gripping a tennis racket, and squeeze gently, coaxing out as much water as you can. Repeat from midpoint to base of tail and on each leg. Blot the kitten's legs, tail, and body with paper towels to absorb as much additional moisture as possible. Then remove the kitten from the sink and wrap it in a towel, which can be warmed in the oven beforehand for your kitten's postbath comfort.

Drying Your Kitten

If your house is warm and you have a shorthair kitten, you can allow the kitten to air dry after a bath. If you would rather not have a wet kitten lying on the carpet or sitting on the furniture, confine your kitten to the bathroom until the kitten dries. Give it water, a toy with which to amuse itself, and a little treat or snack. The nicer you are to the kitten after its bath—and the more special the food treat you give it—the more likely your pet is to remember that baths end pleasantly. After spending an hour confined to a warm room, your kitten should be virtually dry.

Your kitten will be more likely to forgive you for getting it wet if you wrap it in a warm towel after a bath.

You can allow a longhair kitten to air dry, too, as long as you do not mind if your kitten winds up looking like something the cat dragged in. If you do mind, or if your house is a trifle cool, a hair dryer is a more efficient and healthful means of drying a kitten. If you decide to use a hand-held dryer, put two or three drops of natural-tears solution or another moisturizing agent into your kitten's eyes before you begin.

Do not expect your kitten to take any more naturally to hair dryers than to water. In fact, the best time to get your kitten used to the sound and fury of a hair dryer is before you plan to use it. If you dry your own hair with a hair dryer, bring your kitten into the bathroom or bedroom when you dry your hair. If you do not fancy the blow-dried look, put the hair dryer somewhere in the area where you feed your kitten and turn the dryer on just before feeding time. Start the dryer on a low-speed setting before you begin preparing the kitten's food. Leave the dryer running while the kitten eats. If your kitten shies at the sound, leave the dryer running and leave the room for a few minutes. If your kitten refuses to eat, take up the food, turn off the dryer, and try again in a half hour. Eventually your kitten will be hungry enough to eat with the dryer running.

Before applying the hair dryer, put a towel on the surface the kitten will occupy while being dried. Wrist test the temperature of the air coming out of the dryer. The air should not be too hot nor too forceful. The best dryers are the ones with separate speed and temperature controls and quiet-running motors. Some dryers even have a separate control that turns hot air to cool so you can moderate the temperature as you get closer to your kitten.

You may find it more convenient to begin the drying process by placing your kitten in the towel-lined carrier you had prepared for emergencies. If you try this approach, position the dryer so that warm air blows temperately into the carrier through the front door.

Take the kitten out of the carrier after 20 minutes or so, and place the kitten on a table or counter. While directing a stream of warm air into the kitten's coat, comb cautiously. After the hairs in that area have been separated, move to another area of the kitten. If you are attempting this job alone, be sure to use a hair dryer that has a stand into which you can set the dryer, thus leaving your dryer hand free for lifting the kitten while you dry and comb its underbelly. Be sure that the dryer stand is resting on a towel or else as soon as you have the dryer adjusted to the proper angle for drying the kitten's underbelly, the stand will start moving backward of its own accord.

When you have gone over the entire kitten once with the dryer, begin again. This time concentrate on one section of coat at a time. Do not concentrate more than a minute or two on any one section because the heat from the dryer could become uncomfortable for your kitten. To avoid this possibility, keep the dryer moving back and forth above the section on which you are working.

As the coat becomes more dry, use the lift-and-flip technique (see page 82) to aerate the hairs and get them completely dry. Use a toothbrush (or a flea comb) to groom the kitten's face. If you notice that static electricity is raising cain with your kitten's hair, rub a cling-free type anti-static cloth over the kitten's coat to smooth the hair into place.

Routine Ear Care

A kitten's ears are not difficult to keep clean. All you need are a few cotton swabs or cotton balls and some rubbing alcohol, mineral oil, or hydrogen peroxide in a small container. Dip the cotton swabs or cotton balls into the alcohol, oil, or peroxide (the choice is yours) and swab the visible parts of the ear carefully. Do not plunge the cotton swab or cotton ball down into the ear canal any farther than the eye can see, or you might do some damage. If you wish to clean your kitten's lower ear canal, buy a cleaning solution from your veterinarian and follow the instructions faithfully.

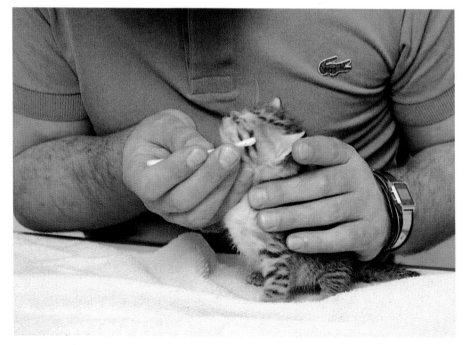

The area around a cat's eyes should be cleaned— carefully— whenever it is dirty.

Chapter 9
The Kitten's Body Works

Unlike dogs, which occur in a multitude of sizes and designs, cats are limited in composition. The difference between the largest breed of cat, the ragdoll, and the smallest breed, the Singapura, is little more than a dozen pounds and less than one square foot at the extreme; and the difference between the longest and the shortest facial profiles among pedigreed cats, namely, between the Siamese and the Persian, is a matter of inches.

Virtually all the disparities between cat breeds—and among dog breeds, too—do not exist because nature has decreed they should. Most breeds and the differences among them were fashioned and preserved by animal fanciers along lines of which nature would not always approve.

For its part, the domestic cat, which has been spared manipulation by humans, is a remarkably homogeneous creature. Predominantly short-haired and often tiger-striped, the domestic cat measures between 12 and 15 inches (30.5–38.1 cm) from its shoulders to the base of its tail and generally weighs between 7 and 10 pounds (3.2–4.5 kg).

The domestic cat's skeleton is confusingly similar to that of the wild cat from which it is descended. The foremost distinguishing features of the domestic cat are a shorter coat, a smaller brain, a slightly broader skull, a steep rise in the premaxillary bones of the upper jaw, and a longer gap between the canine teeth and the premolars of the lower jaw, which gap is occasioned by the smaller-sized teeth of the domestic cat.

The Senses

Sight

Kittens are born blind. Their eyes remain closed from seven to ten days on average. The retina—which is located at the rear of the eye chamber and which contains blood vessels and light-sensitive rods and cones—is not developed completely at birth, and a kitten's vision is poor. Vision improves gradually for about three months, at which time the kitten can see as well as an adult cat.

At maturity, the cat's eyes are a hunter's eyes, roughly 0.75 to 0.875 inch (1.9–2.2 cm) in diameter, set well to the fore, and aimed straight ahead to provide the most acute three-dimensional picture. The ligaments surrounding the lens of the eye allow the lens to bulge forward, in order to focus on objects close at hand, or to flatten out, in order to focus on objects farther away. Nonetheless, cats are somewhat farsighted. They cannot focus well on any object closer than 30 inches (76 cm) away, and their depth of field is in sharpest focus between 7 and 20 feet (2.1–6.1 m).

The cat's eye is a gem that reflects a mysterious luster. Pillowed in cushions of fat, the eye is protected by a pair of eyelids that are almost camouflaged by fur. The eyelids close reflexively if anything touches the cat's eyelashes, whiskers, or eyes. (Cats also possess a third eyelid known as the nictitating membrane or haw. This thin fold of skin, located underneath the eyelid, flicks diagonally upward across the eye, helping to lubricate the cornea. The haw also rises when cats are unwell.)

Most of the cat's eye is surrounded by a dense, white, fibrous membrane called the sclera. The transparent portion of the sclera covering the iris and pupil is known as the cornea. The pupil is the expanding and contracting opening in the iris, which is a contractile, cir-

cular diaphragm that forms the colored portion of the eye. Just behind the iris and pupil is the lens, which is suspended by muscles and ligaments. The chamber behind the lens is filled with a jellylike substance called the vitreous humor.

Kittens, which are born blind, do not open their eyes for seven to ten days, on average.

If the eyes are the windows of the soul, kittens are among the most soulful creatures on earth.

At the rear of the eye chamber is the retina. Part of the retina is backed by the light-reflecting tapetum lucidum, and part is backed by the dark tapetum nigrum. The optic nerve, made of sensory fibers, transmits signals from the retina to the brain. The short focal length of the eye—a product of the curvature of the cornea and the lens and of the shortness of the cat's eyeball as well—gives the cat a wide-angle-camera view of the world compared to the more narrow view afforded by the human eye.

Light stimulates a chemical reaction in millions of special cells in the retina, setting off impulses in the optic nerve fibers. The pattern formed by these electrical signals creates images on the retina. These are transmitted via the optic nerve to the visual area of the brain, where they reach the cat's consciousness.

Cats can see moving objects better than stationary ones because specific cells in the cat's brain respond to movement. Thus, cats freeze when they are hunting so that their prey will not notice them.

Although they cannot see in total darkness, cats are most efficient gleaners of light. Their lenses and corneas are larger, relative to the other components of their eyes, than is usual in other species. Moreover, the setting of their lenses—farther back in a cat's than in a human's eyeball—helps to project onto the retina of the cat's eye an image that is five times brighter than the image projected onto a human retina. Cats are able to see in light that is at least six times more dim than the light in which humans can see.

Cats adjust to varying degrees of light by narrowing or dilating their pupils. In brightest sunlight the cat's pupils are closed completely except for two tiny openings at the top and bottom of the pupil. In dim light the pupil may be as much as 0.5 inch (1.3 cm) wide.

At night, cats' eyes glitter with an unearthly glow, a reflection of the light striking the mirrorlike tapetum lucidum, which lines most of the surface of the back of the retina. The color reflected by the tapetum lucidum varies with the color of the cat's eye. Yellow- or orange-eyed cats reflect a greenish glow; blue-eyed cats reflect a reddish gleam.

Cats are not color-blind. They can distinguish red from blue and both these colors from white. Yet researchers believe that green, yellow, and white all register as a pale shade of white to the cat.

Hearing

The cat's auditory world includes rustlings and reverberations that are more faint and high-pitched than the sounds humans can hear. Because the upper limit of a cat's hearing range is one and a half octaves higher than is a human's, cats can detect the ultrasonic calls of rodents. Humans—thankfully, one supposes—cannot. (The upper limit of a cat's hearing range is higher also than a dog's, although dogs and humans can detect lower sounds than do cats.)

A cat's power of auditory discrimination is not so great as a human's. From a distance of 3 feet (0.9 m), two different sources of sound must be at least 3 inches (7.6 cm) apart before cats can discriminate between them. From the same distance, humans are able to discriminate between two sounds that are only 0.33 inch (0.8 cm) apart. Cats, however, are able to ignore the sound of their owners' voices from virtually any distance.

The pinna, or ear flap, is equipped with more than a dozen muscles that confer upon it great mobility. A cat can rotate its pinnae through 180 degrees and can incline them toward the source of a sound. The pinnae gather sound waves and funnel them down through the external auditory canal to the eardrum.

In addition to gathering sound so that a cat can interpret a message, the pinnae enable a cat to send messages, too. There is no mistaking, for example, the message intended by a cat when its ears are drawn back.

Not every component of a cat's ear is devoted to the gathering, transcription, and translation of sound waves. The vestibular apparatus, located in the inner ear, monitors the cat's balance and alignment. Composed of three fluid-filled, semicircular canals and two larger chambers, all of which

are filled with millions of tiny hairs, the vestibular apparatus relays information regarding the cat's movement and orientation in space to the brain. In no small part responsible for the cat's vaunted sense of balance, the vestibular apparatus sends signals to the brain whenever the hairs in its chambers move.

In the utricle and saccule, the large chambers of the vestibular apparatus, tiny crystals of calcium carbonate (chalk) press down on the hairs at the bottom of the chambers to relay information to the brain regarding the cat's vertical orientation. In the three semicircular canals, the hairs project into flaps of tissue. Whenever the cat moves its head, the fluid in the semicircular canals sloshes about, moving the hairs in the canals and relaying

Could this kitten sound as unhappy as it looks?

information to the brain. Because the three semicircular canals are arranged at right angles to one another, they can signal the direction and acceleration of movement.

Taste

The cat's tongue, a pink, flexible rasp, is dotted with tiny, prickly knobs called papillae. The filiform papillae in the center of the tongue are backward facing hooks, which the cat uses to hold food, to scrape bones clean, or to polish its fur. The fungiform or mushroom-shaped papillae along the front and side edges of the tongue contain taste buds, as do the four or six large vallate or cup-shaped papillae at the back of the tongue.

The kitten's tongue is an all-purpose tool that is, in addition, very sensitive.

Researchers employed by cat food manufacturers have gotten the cat's tongue to reveal much about taste reactions and preferences among felines. Of the four basic taste dimensions in mammals—acid, bitter, salt, and sweet—the latter is nonsignificant to cats, a fact revealed by the absence of conduction fibers for the sweet taste in the glossopharyngeal nerve between the tongue and the cerebrum. Cats are virtually alone among mammals in exhibiting no significant reaction to sweets, a phenomenon that is not surprising in a true carnivore like the cat.

Taste is a close neighbor to smell, and both are chemical senses. A cat unable to smell for whatever reason often refuses to eat. Because of the association between taste and smell, cats sometimes smell with their mouths open, an activity known as "flehming." A cat in full flehmen traps airborne molecules of scent on its tongue, then presses the tongue against the opening of its vomeronasal or Jacobson's organ, an 0.5 inch (1.3 cm), cigar-shaped sac located in the roof of the cat's mouth. A narrow tube leads from the vomeronasal organ to a spot just above the cat's front teeth. (Humans have a vestigial, nonfunctioning trace of this organ in their hard palates.) The flehmen reaction in cats may be triggered by catnip, a stranger in the house, a female in season in the yard next door, or other interesting scents.

Smell

Like the senses of taste and touch, the cat's sense of smell has been shown through anatomical evidence to be present at birth. One-day-old kittens have demonstrated an ability to distinguish between salted and nonsalted liquids. Indeed, throughout their lives, cats are greatly sensitive to the taste of water. They, more so than humans, one suspects, can tell the difference between bottled water products, whereas human perception of such differences may be confined mainly to observations regarding price.

Often, when neonatal kittens are moved from a familiar nest, they begin to cry because they are distressed that the smell of the new nest is different from the smell of the old, familiar one. Kittens do not settle in the new nest until their mother rejoins them and reassures them, by her smell, that all is well. (The sense of smell is thought to be responsible, too, for a kitten's inclination to return to the same nipple each time it nurses.)

In a real sense cats read with their noses, sniffing studiously all new objects, persons, other animals, and food they encounter; but there is more to the sense of smell than meets the nose. Behind the cat's nose lies a maze of bones and cavities. When cats breathe, air passing through this maze is warmed and moistened. Part of the air is channeled across the olfactory mucosa, which covers a relatively large area, 3 to 6 square inches (20–40 square cm), in the cat's nasal lining. This is nearly twice the size of the olfactory mucosa of rabbits, which are comparable in size to the cat, or of

Cats see with their eyes, but they read with their noses.

humans, who are much larger. The olfactory mucosa contains a complex arrangement of cells. The most important are the 200 million olfactory cells, which are sensitive to volatile airborne substances.

In addition, a cat's sense of smell is supercharged by the subethmoid shelf in the cat's nose. After a cat sniffs at something purposefully, the sniffed air is not expelled when the cat exhales. Instead of moving through the nasal passages, into the lungs, and back out through the nasal passages, sniffed air and the scent molecules it carries remain in the cat's nose above the subethmoid shelf so that the air can be "read" more closely by the cat.

The order of difference between a cat's sense of smell and ours is considerable. We can smell an unpeeled clove of garlic faintly from a close perspective. Yet we smell garlic keenly when it is crackling in olive oil in the skillet. The cat can smell garlic at that high-impact level before we get it out of the shopping bag. Thus, a cat's sense of smell enables it to tell far more about the age, sex, and health of other cats than we humans, with our feeble senses of smell, can imagine.

Touch

The cat's sense of touch conveys sensations of pressure, cold, warmth, and pain. A newborn kitten employs its sense of touch, more specifically its knack for detecting warmth, to find its way to its mother in the nest. This heat-sensing ability continues to develop as the kitten matures. The heat receptors in an adult cat's nose are sensitive enough to detect differences in temperature as small as 0.9°F (0.5°C).

Although warmth and cold receptors are present all over a cat's body, the cat is relatively insensitive to high and low temperatures except on its face and paws. For example, cats do not react to heat at temperatures below 126°F (52°C) on the average, whereas humans feel discomfort when their skin temperature reaches 112°F (44°C).

The most sensitive touch receptors are located in a cat's whiskers and its paws, especially in its forepaws. A cat's whiskers, or vibrissae, contain bundles of nerves that send impulses to the brain along the same channel used by the eyes. Whiskers are sensitive to contact and to movements in the air. If you touch the whiskers over a cat's eyes, the cat will blink. Whiskers also are used to gauge the size of an opening a cat is investigating and to help a cat "see" objects in the dark by detecting the slight eddies that these objects create in the air around them.

The importance of a cat's forepaws as a source of tactile information is suggested by the size of the area of the cat's brain that receives messages from the forepaws. In fact, all four of the cat's paw pads are extremely sensitive. They provide information about the texture of objects and about their temperature as well. Some people believe that a cat's paw pads can detect vibrations, which would explain why some cats appear to be able to "hear" through their feet. (If a person were to crawl across the floor or backyard, the sensations recorded by the hands would be somewhat similar to those recorded by a cat's paws.)

Besides transmitting painful impulses to the brain, the cat's sense of touch conveys pleasurable sensations, too. A mother washes her kittens with her sandpapery tongue and moves them toward her in the nest with her paws. From this, kittens learn to associate certain kinds of touches with a caring attitude. Later in life adult cats make the same association upon receiving attentive—or even absent-minded—stroking from a human hand, which recreates the pleasure a kitten felt when it was licked by its mother in the nest.

Petting and grooming are said to reduce tension by slowing down a cat's heart rate. Perhaps this is why a cat frequently will start to wash in situations that evoke doubt or stress.

The sense of touch is employed also when a cat chooses a place to sleep. Cats like warm, soft fabrics and often will refuse to stay on the lap of someone wearing a cold or slippery dress or trousers or clothing made of synthetic fiber. Not surprisingly, cats always seek out warm sleeping spots (the crooks of human knees are a favorite site). As their faces are the most cold-sensitive

parts of their bodies, cats are quick to curl up into a ball when they are cold, using their tails as mufflers for keeping their faces warm.

Most small objects are fair prey to a kitten.

Muscles

Striped (voluntary)

From the first time a kitten paddles toward its mother, it seeks to command its voluntary muscles, so called because they operate under the brain's conscious command. Voluntary muscles are also called skeletal muscles because their chief function is to move the kitten's skeleton, and hence the kitten, from place to place. In addition, the voluntary muscles are sometimes called striped or striated muscles because their appearance is characterized by latitudinal stripes.

Whatever they are called, the skeletal muscles enable a kitten to

selves, hurling the kitten temporarily beyond gravity's dominion.

The kitten's skeleton is decorated in wreaths of skeletal muscles, more than 500 weight-pulling garlands of muscle in all. Each skeletal muscle comprises numerous bundles of long, cylindrical cells known as fibers. These fibers, from 1 to 40 millimeters long and from 10 to 100 micrometers wide, are about the size of a human hair.

Skeletal muscles receive electrical impulses from the brain after it has processed information provided by the senses. The motor cortex, which commands movement, and the cerebellum, which coordinates balance, are the shop stewards in the brain that issue work orders for the cat's skeletal muscles.

Depending on the kind of action it wants to initiate, the brain will send either of two electrical messages to the motor end nerve attached to each unit of skeletal muscle fiber. Tonic stimulation (or low electrical frequency in long bursts) governs ongoing activity such as paw washing. Phasic stimulation (or high electrical frequencies in short bursts) activates muscle fibers when sudden action, such as racing across the living room in pursuit of a thrown toy, is required.

Muscles display a full-speed-ahead, all-or-nothing approach to life. Thus, the power of a contraction is governed by the number of muscle fibers that are ordered to contract, not by the extent to which they are ordered to contract. If the

scrimmage with its littermates for a place in the food line, to knead contentedly against its mother's belly, to crawl, wobble, stand, totter, fall, right itself, ratchet its head about uncertainly, fall, rise again, and, finally, walk. Secured to the skeleton by tendons, skeletal muscles always are arranged in pairs—antagonists and protagonists that work in cooperative opposition to each other.

When a kitten jumps, for example, it crouches on its heels by contracting two muscles: the hamstring, a flexor muscle located behind the thighbone, and the tibialis, a flexor muscle located in front of the tibia and fibula bones. At that point the corresponding extensor muscles that were stretched while the hamstring and tibialis were contracting, contract powerfully them-

brain estimates that only two thirds of a muscle's power is needed to perform some action, only two thirds of that muscle's fibers will receive the call to arms.

Smooth (involuntary)

Both chapters of the United Muscular Workers Union—voluntary and involuntary—begin to form about 11 or 12 days after fertilization when a kitten embryo is but a hopeful confederation of cells scarcely 0.20 inch (4 mm) long. Involuntary (or smooth) muscles, which are not consciously controlled by the kitten, are found in working-class locations such as the alimentary canal and the inner spaces of the urogenital and respiratory systems of the cat. Smooth muscles are also on the job in the walls of the arterioles, helping to determine arteriole size and, thereby, to help maintain blood pressure.

Whereas skeletal muscles occur most often in bundles, smooth muscle fibers are arranged usually in sheets, small groups, or—especially in the dermis—singly. And even though smooth muscle fibers lie parallel to one another, they are not arranged in the lock-step, close-order drill of the skeletal muscles. The tip of one smooth muscle fiber, for example, often will be found cheek by jowl with the midsection of another fiber in the same sheet. That is why smooth muscles do not exhibit latitudinal stripes as do skeletal muscles.

Not only are they imprecise in their orientation, smooth muscle fibers also are smaller than are skeletal muscle fibers. The latter range from 1 to 40 millimeters in length and from 10 to 100 micrometers in width. Smooth muscles generally are 0.2 millimeters long and 6 micrometers wide. Understandably, the contractions made by smooth muscles are not so large as are the contractions made by skeletal muscles.

Like the guitar and bass in a jazz combo, smooth and skeletal muscles play their parts in the body's harmonious composition. The smooth muscles keep the beat, marking time like a metronome, whereas the skeletal muscles play improvisations on the melody, eventually lending grace, style, and majesty to the movements of the kitten.

Skeleton

Officially classified as connective tissue designed to bear weight, bone lends definition and support to the kitten's body and protection to its internal organs. There are 244 bones in the feline skeleton—from the stately, immobile sections of the neurocranium to the nimble, trinket-like phalanges in the toes.

Cartilage, bone's pearl-handled ally in the skeletal system, performs several important functions as well. It coats the ends of bones in movable joints, allowing them to rub against each other with minimal friction and wear. Cartilage also connects the ribs to the sternum, forming a safety deposit box for the heart and lungs. What's more, cartilage supports the epiglottis, larynx, trachea, bronchi, and external ear.

The skeletal system begins developing in the kitten embryo before a female gives any signs that she is pregnant. About 11 days after fertilization has occurred, the embryo starts to attach itself to the uterine wall. At the same time, cells begin to matriculate to one of three concentric layers forming in the embryo—ectoderm, mesoderm, or endoderm. Through this process, known as differentiation, cells become structurally and functionally unique.

When differentiated cells continue to multiply after reaching their destinations in the embryo, they do so in kind, but they are still subject to further modification by genetic mandate. Some of the cells in the mesoderm, for example, develop into mesenchymal cells; and these, in turn, develop into chondroblasts, which give rise to cartilage, or into osteoblasts, which give rise to bone.

As chondroblasts reproduce, they build a cartilaginous model of the skeleton that will someday inhabit the mature cat. By and large, the majority of bone in the adult skeleton will be formed within and upon this slight, delicate precursor. One day the skeleton will collaborate with muscle to transform the cat into a statement of power and grace (or klutzy charm); but in the young embryo, the skeleton—so decisive in its prime—is only a pliant approximation of its future self.

Bone can be cataloged into three classes according to shape: long, flat, and irregular. The radius and ulna in the front legs, as well as the tibia and fibula in the hind legs are long bones. The scapula, or shoulder blade, is a flat bone. So are the bones of the skull and face. The metatarsals and metacarpals in the feet are irregular bones.

Cats reach skeletal maturity sometime between eight months and one year of age. At that point, what you see is what you are going to see. Growth plates—the cartilaginous layers situated between the shafts and the ends of bones—do not normally close until a cat is one year old. Sometimes growth plates remain open longer. If they do, there is potential for growth, but significant bone growth beyond the first year of a cat's life is rare.

Part protein, part mineral, mostly water, the skeletal system of the cat is a bona fide marvel. Practically maintenance free, it is almost injury free, too, because automobiles, the major source of broken bones in cats, seldom venture indoors. (And bone, once broken, even exhibits a good-natured inclination to effect its own repair within reasonable limits.) In addition, bone disease, like bone injury, is an infrequent problem with cats, who are less prone than are some companion animals to osteoarthritis, rheumatoid arthritis, and the other infirmities that come with the dismal territory of old age. Indeed, like the finest of silent partners, bone makes its presence felt in the cat without being seen or heard.

Intelligence

Although writers from Plutarch in the first century to Montaigne in the sixteenth have remarked on the cleverness of animals, the subject of animal intelligence was declared so much hogwash by René Descartes, the father of modern philosophy, in the mid-seventeenth century. From then until the publication of Charles Darwin's *On the Origin of Species* in 1859, animals were considered "beast machines": dumb, hidebound creatures of habit and heredity that reacted to their surroundings, but never reflected on them, much less on themselves.

On the Origin of Species, which sold out the day it was published, rattled the cages of the scientific establishment; and for the half century following the Darwinian revolution, psychologists and biologists were eager to study the mental experiences—and by extension, the intelligence—of animals. This helped open the door to behaviorism, which closed the door, around 1920, on any suggestions that animals—and people, too, according to many behaviorists—are mentally capable of anything more sophisticated than reacting to external stimuli.

Though pre-Darwinian attitudes regarding animal intelligence unfortunately inform much of the populace today, roughly 25 years ago, scientists began to ask whether human beings alone—among all the earth's inhabitants—possess the capacities for thought and self-consciousness. And if so, what is the proof for these unique, human capabilities? And wherein lies their source? If not, what evidence is there that other creatures can think? And which nonhumans are the most intelligent thinkers?

Manifestations of intelligence abound in the animal kingdom. One example comes from Marine World. To enlist the cooperation of captive dolphins in removing litter that had blown into their pool, trainer Jim Mullen devised a trash-for-fish plan whereby dolphins were paid according to scale for every scrap of refuse they retrieved. The system worked swimmingly, but Mullen noticed that one dolphin, Mr. Spock, soon had a virtual monopoly on trash hauling. Curious about Spock's success, Mullen watched through an underwater observation window while an assistant directed a pool-cleaning session. Thus did Mullen learn that the enterprising Spock was hoarding paper bags full of trash beneath a platform and was cashing them in at feeding time.

Another manifestation of thought among animals was provided by a young male baboon. One day this youngster observed an adult female baboon digging roots from the cracked, dry earth. He looked around after a moment and, seeing

Cats like to study their reflections in the water. They also like to study the movements of fish.

no other animals in sight, screamed bloody murder as though he had been attacked. His mother came running, saw the alleged offending female, over which she held dominance, and swiftly uprooted her. The sly, mendacious male then helped himself to a free lunch.

Were either of these behaviors exhibited by a young child, psychologists would consider them manifestations of the child's developing intelligence; but since the agents in question were not human, most members of the scientific community for most of this and preceding centuries would have explained these actions in terms of conditioning, stimulus-response theory, hereditary instinct, or some other mechanistic paradigm. The dolphin and the baboon—like the dog that waxes euphoric at the sight of a lead or the cat that zooms toward the kitchen like a heat-seeking missile at the sound of a can being opened—are given an *A* for promptness of response, but no credit for anything more. To suggest otherwise in scientific company—or even to raise certain questions—has been to risk being regarded with the condescension and amusement usually accorded someone who shows up at a black-tie dinner in a Hawaiian shirt.

Fortunately, some scientists have begun to rethink the notion of animal intelligence. Their conclusions were summed up nicely in 1987 in *New Scientist* magazine. "It is highly improbable that [animal] brains anatomically and physiologically so much more similar than dissimilar to our own don't generate a broadly comparable pattern of consciousness. No appreciation of poetry, perhaps. Not much feel for the works of the Impressionists, maybe. Little in the way of mathematical skills, I dare swear. Small thought for the prospects of eternal salvation or damnation, I'll warrant. But no fear, no pleasure, no frustration, no anticipation of habitual delights or apprehension of unpleasant happenings or disappointments? Rubbish!"

And no thinking? Rubbish again.

People who believe that animals possess intelligence often believe that one species possesses more than another. The cat, which has a 1- to 2-ounce (29–57 g) brain with perhaps 10 billion neurons, has been ranked somewhere between a gerbil and a marmoset on a cerebral development chart, but it is difficult at best to compare intelligence across species.

Each species is born with a predisposition to learn what it needs to learn in order to survive. Dogs, for example, are pack animals, thus they are highly social because the ability to respond to social reinforcement is important to living in a pack. This sociability makes dogs easier to train, and because they are easier to train, dogs are often considered more intelligent than are cats. Cats living in the wild, however, are essentially solitary or, at their most gregarious, colonial animals. They do not have a complex social organization, nor do they hunt in packs. Therefore, some kinds of learning are not important to cats, so they do not learn in the same way that dogs do. This does not mean that cats are less intelligent than are dogs.

Chapter 10
The Healthy Kitten

Cats can see moving objects better than stationary ones because specific cells in the cat's brain respond to movement.

Kittens that are sick are often listless or cranky. They also may begin to neglect their litter pans. Any deviations from a kitten's normal behavior that persist for more than a day should be cause for concern and a consultation with the veterinarian.

Favorable Signs

Signs of good health are evident in the way that kittens look, behave, and groom themselves. Healthy kittens have bright eyes, cool, slightly damp noses, and ears that are free of dirt and wax. Their gums are neither pale nor inflamed. Their bodies are taut and well muscled, not paunchy or perilously thin. Healthy kittens take immaculate care of their coats, which are not marred by bald patches, scabs, or flea dirt. The area below a healthy kitten's tail is free of dried waste, and the fur on the hindquarters is not discolored.

Even healthy kittens spend inspiring amounts of time asleep, as many as 14 to 18 hours a day, but otherwise they are busy, alert, and unrelentingly curious. They are affectionate toward their owners, careful about their appearance, and keenly interested in life and mealtimes. They are, to be sure, the cat's pajamas.

Trouble Signs

Perhaps the first sign that a kitten is not feeling well is a lack of interest in food. If a kitten skips one meal or makes a languid, desultory sniff at the plate, nibbles a moment, then walks away, you need not assume there is anything wrong. All kittens go off their feed occasionally, but the kitten that misses two consecutive meals probably would benefit from a trip to a veterinarian—especially if its temperature is elevated or if it presents any other symptoms of illness.

Some signs of illness, however, are significant enough to occasion a straightforward trip to the veterinarian, as soon as you have called to say what is ailing your kitten and to find out if you may come over right away. The following list enumerates some of those emergency symptoms. Do not consider the list exhaustive and do not mistake it for a diagnostic tool.

You should take your kitten to the veterinarian at once if your kitten:

• Has a deep wound or one that is still bleeding after pressure has been applied to it.

• Seems drowsy after eating a foreign substance.

• Stops breathing after chewing on a plant.

• Has a temperature above 105°F (40.6°C).

• Exhibits a sudden weakness in the hindquarters that makes it difficult to walk.

• Has a red, ulcerated sore on its lips or any other part of its body.

• Develops an abscess that is warm and painful to the touch.

• Has a runny nose accompanied by a temperature above 103.5°F (39.5°C), pale gums, or weakness.

• Shows any evidence of trauma accompanied by shortness of breath, a temperature of 103.5°F (39.5°C) or more, pale gums, or lethargy.

• Vomits and appears lethargic, attempts to urinate frequently, and has a temperature of 103.5°F (39.5°C) or more, and/or bloody stools.

• Has diarrhea, bloody feces, a temperature, or is vomiting.

• Is constipated and strains at the stool while failing to defecate.

You should call your veterinarian for advice and an appointment if your kitten:

• Has abnormally thin stools and an elevated temperature.

• Has a temperature between 103.5 and 105°F (39.5–40.6°C) and other signs of illness.

• Begins drinking more water than usual and urinating excessively, has diarrhea, is lethargic, or has an elevated temperature.

• Has a decreased appetite, is coughing, vomiting, or has diarrhea.

• Exhibits general lameness in any leg for more than two days.

• Develops a swelling that is warm and painful to the touch.

• Has a runny nose accompanied by lethargy, pus in the eye, or rapid breathing.

• Has a cough accompanied by an elevated temperature, difficult breathing, and lack of energy.

• Has foul-smelling breath, is drinking water excessively, eating frequently, urinating frequently, yet appears lethargic.

• Has diarrhea accompanied by dehydration. (A kitten is dehydrated if you take a pinch of skin from over its spine between your thumb and forefinger, lift the skin away from its body, and let go of the skin, which then does not spring back immediately into place.)

Preventive Health Care

A study published by the American Veterinary Medical Association (AVMA) in 1992 revealed that 62 percent of the cat owning house-

After you have acquired a kitten, you should take it to the veterinarian to have it examined.

holds in the United States had sought veterinary care for their cats during the preceding year. This represented a mere 5 percent increase in the number of cat owning households that had sought veterinary care for their cats in 1987, the last year in which the AVMA had gathered such information. (There had been a 26 percent increase in the number of cat owning households that had sought veterinary care for their cats between 1983 and 1987.) Unfortunately, the AVMA study reveals that nearly two out of every five cats in the United States still receives no medical attention, not even for an annual booster shot and physical examination.

The AVMA data reminds us that the joy of owning a kitten or a cat is accompanied by certain responsibilities. Owners should provide their kittens with prompt, competent, and kindly medical care when necessary; a safe, clean, comfortable, stimulating indoor environment; a balanced, nutritious, invigorating diet; a yearly examination and booster shots; and habitual, caring companionship.

The centerpiece and the measure of preventive health care is the annual physical examination and the booster shots that are normally administered at that time. The first annual trip, of course, should be scheduled shortly after you acquire your kitten.

In the basic examination the veterinarian will inspect your kitten's coat, looking to see if it exhibits the softness, sheen, and texture that are signs of good health or if it shows any indication of broken hairs, scales, fleas, flea dirt, or ringworm that are signs of trouble. The veterinarian may also test for dehydration. In addition, the veterinarian will look at your kitten's eyes and ears, examine its teeth, listen to its heart and lungs, and palpate its kidneys and liver. Unless there is a reason why a kitten should not receive them, the veterinarian will then administer the appropriate vaccinations. (The final item of a kitten's initial inspection is the fecal examination, in which a stool sample is assayed for various kinds of worms.)

Vaccinations

While they are in the womb, kittens are protected against disease by dint of the immunity they inherit from their mothers. After they are born, kittens are usually protected against disease by antibodies in their mothers' milk. This passive, or inherited immunity, lasts until kittens are roughly eight weeks old. Because passive immunity interferes with kittens' ability to produce their own antibodies, kittens generally are not vaccinated until they reach eight weeks of age.

The genius of the vaccination procedure is that it stimulates the body's immune defenses without causing disease. When a kitten is vaccinated, a small quantity of vaccine designed to protect against one or more feline disorders is introduced into the kitten's bloodstream. Immunization, the desired result of vaccination, is the process by which the immune system recognizes foreign proteins (or antigens) in a vaccine. Once the immune system recognizes these intruders, it manufactures protective proteins (or antibodies) and white blood cells that ingest and remove foreign material from the body.

That initial disease-fighting response, which is low grade and not entirely effective, begins about five to ten days after a kitten has been vaccinated. A second vaccination, which instigates a more vigorous, long-lasting response, is given three to four weeks later. Most veterinarians also recommend a third and even a fourth vaccination at four-week intervals.

Vaccines can be introduced into a kitten's body in one of three ways: intramuscularly, intranasally, or subcutaneously. The choice of a vaccine and the way it is administered are influenced by the kitten's age and health.

Killed vaccine: A killed vaccine cannot cause disease or replicate itself inside a kitten. A veterinarian confident of obtaining effective immunity by using a killed vaccine generally will do so because killed vaccines possess greater stability than other vaccines and offer maximum safety. A veterinarian who suspects that a kitten might be immunosuppressed (i.e., might have a weakened disease-fighting system) also would use a killed vaccine because it does not contain live virus.

Modified-live vaccines: Modified-live vaccines continue to replicate in a kitten or cat. A veterinarian who seeks to achieve a faster, more broad-based, immune-system response will choose a modified-live vaccine. Moreover, modified-live vaccines also confer a relatively long-term immunity.

Intramuscular or subcutaneous inoculation: Killed or modified-live vaccines can be administered intramuscularly or subcutaneously. The latter route is preferred by most veterinarians, not because subcutaneous injections provide any physiologic advantage in invoking an immune-system response, but simply because they are more comfortable for the kitten. If for some reason a veterinarian wants to get the vaccine into the bloodstream more quickly, he or she will give the kitten an intramuscular injection.

Sydney, the kitten, is giving her medical history to her veterinarian.

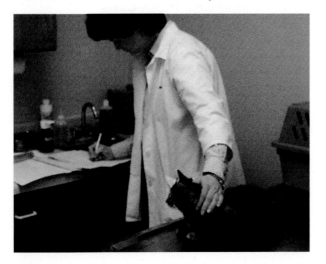

Intranasal inoculation: Vaccines are administered intranasally when it is necessary to vaccinate against the upper respiratory viruses that enter the body through the nasal passages. Intranasal inoculations, which are limited to modified live vaccines, produce a local immune response on the linings of the nasal passages. This response, which can be important in stopping the early phase of infection at the source, may not be produced as readily from intramuscular or subcutaneous inoculations.

Most kitten vaccinations are administered in a three-way injection designed to confer immunity against feline panleukopenia, feline viral rhinotracheitis, and feline calicivirus. Fewer than 1 percent of healthy kittens vaccinated in this manner at the proper age with the right dose of a properly stored vaccine will fail to produce an immune response. The same can be said of the rabies vaccine, but not of the feline leukemia virus vaccine.

Like failure to develop immunity, severe allergic reactions to vaccination are rare. If they occur, the kitten should be taken back to the veterinarian at once. It is a good idea, therefore, to schedule vaccinations for early in the day so that if you have to rush a kitten back to the vet, the office still will be open.

No matter how advanced the technology for producing vaccines might become, a vaccination is only as good as the exam that preceded it. Indeed, next to the vaccine, the most important factor in developing immunization is the veterinarian, who by training and experience is best qualified to judge when a kitten is healthy enough to be vaccinated. For this reason, if you buy kittens from breeders who vaccinate kittens themselves, you should ask if the breeder has the kittens examined by a veterinarian before they receive their first shots. If the breeder does not, you might want to consider buying a kitten from someone who does.

External Parasites

Parasites are living organisms that reside in or on other living organisms (called hosts), feeding on blood, lymph cells, or tissue. Parasites come in two operating modes: internal parasites (or endoparasites) that dwell inside their hosts, and external parasites (or ectoparasites) that haunt the surface of their hosts.

The external parasites that might bedevil your kitten include fleas, ticks, flies, lice, larvae, and mites. In addition to damaging skin tissue, this motley crew of insects and arachnids may transmit deleterious bacteria and menacing viruses to your kitten. If external parasites are present in sufficient quantities, they can leave their hosts devoid of energy, weaken their resistance to infection and disease, and infect them with a number of diseases or parasitic worms.

If your kitten has skin lesions, hair loss, itching, redness, dandruff, scaling, growths of thickened skin, or an unpleasant odor, chances are it is harboring some kind of external parasite. Should your kitten exhibit any of these symptoms, take the kitten to the veterinarian for a diagnosis. Depending on the kind of parasite your kitten is hosting, it may have to be isolated from other cats and treated with parasiticidal dips, powders, ointments, and shampoos.

Internal Parasites

There are four types of internal parasites that prosper in kittens: protozoa, nematodes, cestodes, and trematodes.

Protozoa: Protozoa are usually one-celled organisms that may contain specialized structures for feeding and locomotion. The protozoan most familiar to cat owners is *Toxoplasma gondii*. It can cause retinal lesions, calcified lesions in the brain, which are sometimes fatal, or water in the brain cavity of newborn infants whose mothers were infected by *Toxoplasma* during pregnancy. Children infected by *Toxoplasma* postnatally may develop a rash, flulike symptoms, heart disease, pneumonia, retinal lesions, and a fatal central nervous system infection.

To avoid *Toxoplasma* infection, pregnant women should not clean litter pans, or they should wear disposable rubber gloves if they do.

Children, of course, should not be allowed to play near litter pans.

Nematodes: Nematodes somewhat resemble earthworms. The nematodes that most often trouble kittens are roundworms and hookworms, whose presence can be detected through a stool-sample analysis.

Cestodes (or tapeworms): Tapeworms, which are carried by fleas, cannot be detected by stool-sample analysis. Tapeworms are best identified by the old-fashioned, low-tech way—by lifting a cat's tail and peering studiously at its anus. During this examination, you are looking for small, white tapeworm segments that look like grains of rice.

Trematodes: Trematodes are tiny flukes that live in the small intestines of their hosts. Kittens generally become infested with trematodes after dining on raw fish, frogs, or small rodents. It is no fluke that kittens who are kept indoors do not suffer from this kind of worm.

Despite their repugnance worms are not difficult to eliminate. If your kitten's stool sample indicates that the kitten needs to be dewormed, use a product prescribed by your veterinarian, and be sure to use it according to instructions.

Dental Problems

Kittens have 26 teeth. Adult cats have 30. The adult cat's margin of dental victory is provided by its four molars, which kittens do not have. Molars are the teeth located nearest to the throat. There are two upper molars, one on each side of the mouth, and two lower molars, similarly placed.

A kitten's teeth are known as deciduous teeth (from the Latin *deciduus,* meaning "tending to fall"). Also known as baby teeth (from the English preference for shorter words), the deciduous teeth are smaller and more slender than the adult cat's teeth.

The incisors are the first baby teeth to appear. They are the 12 tiny teeth—six upper and six lower—located in the front of the mouth. They begin to erupt (emerge) when a kitten is 11 to 15 days old.

The next kitten teeth to emerge are the four canine teeth, which are the large, fanglike models situated

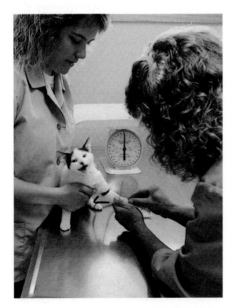

"This is going to hurt me more than it's going to hurt you guys."

on either side of the upper and lower incisors. The canine teeth emerge between 17 and 19 days after a kitten is born.

The last kitten teeth to emerge are the ten premolars, located behind the upper and lower canines. The premolars make their appearance between 37 and 60 days after birth.

When kittens are three and a half to four months old, they begin to lose their baby teeth. Their permanent teeth should all be in place by the time the kittens are six months of age.

A cat's teeth should be white and clean, and its breath, while it lacks the freshness of strawberries and cream, should not smell like freshly scattered fertilizer either. The gums and tissues of a kitten's mouth should be pink, but for the black pigment spots that some kittens have on their gums.

Few kittens suffer from dental problems, but for the occasional kitten whose baby teeth do not fall out by the time their adult teeth emerge. By the time they are two years old, however, most cats are plagued to some degree by oral disease. Soft cat foods do not help to wear away existing plaque: the sticky combination of bacteria, food particles, and saliva that is constantly forming and hardening on our cats' teeth. What's more, soft foods are rich in sugars that promote the development of plaque.

Dry cat foods, though they help to reduce plaque somewhat, also contribute to its buildup. Dry foods are made primarily of grain products. These contain carbohydrates that stick to the teeth and act as compost for the bacteria that is plaque's main ingredient.

Unremoved plaque hardens into calculus (tartar) and intrudes itself between the teeth and gums, creating a tiny sinkhole in which bacteria multiply. These bacteria invade the gingiva (gum), causing it to become inflamed, to swell, and to bleed when probed. This condition, known as gingivitis, is reversible if treated early in its development. If not, it escalates into periodontitis: ulceration of the gums and erosion of the alveolar bone, which holds the teeth in place. Periodontitis is not reversible, and if it is not controlled, the gums and the alveolar bone eventually become so eroded that the teeth fall out. (Gingivitis also can be caused by viruses such as feline calicivirus and feline leukemia virus.)

To check for signs of gingivitis, gently but firmly steady your cat's head with one hand and lift its upper lip along one side of its mouth with the other hand. Look closely at your pet's teeth and gums. Repeat this procedure on the other side and in the front of its mouth. Then inspect the bottom teeth in the same fashion. If your cat's gums look pink, feel firm, and adhere snugly to its teeth, you can assume its teeth are in good health. Pale gums are a warning that a cat may be bleeding internally or suffering from anemia or from any of a number of systemic diseases. A raw-looking, red line along the gums just above the teeth is a sign of gingivitis—and a warning that you should make an appointment to have your veterinarian check your cat's teeth. (More serious gingivitis is accompanied by drooling and bad breath.)

Because most cats are dental-phobic, your cat will have to be placed under general anesthetic in order for the veterinarian to remove accumulated plaque and tartar from the cat's teeth. The vet also will plane your cat's teeth. Planing, which is similar to deep scaling in humans, smooths the root surfaces of the teeth, making it more difficult for plaque to adhere to them. Finally, the vet will polish your cat's teeth and roots and perhaps apply a fluoride treatment to hinder the growth of bacteria, harden tooth enamel, desensitize dentin and pulp (the sensitive layers beneath the tooth enamel), and help reduce bone and tooth destruction.

Brushing Your Kitten's Teeth

Like any other change in a cat's life, the introduction of tooth brushing can be an occasion of stress. Therefore, you should introduce this process by playing a game of "See the Kitty's Teeth" each day. In the middle of a grooming session

steady your cat's head with one hand, lift its lip with the other hand, and have a look at its teeth. You can begin with the top or the bottom teeth, it does not matter. The idea is to get your cat used to your touching its mouth. During and after this game inspection, be certain to reassure and praise your cat. This may be all the reinforcement your cat needs. If not, give it a treat.

After a week or so of "See Kitty's Teeth" you can progress to "Touch the Kitty's Teeth." While you are lifting your cat's lip and checking out its mouth, rub a finger along its teeth. Your cat may tolerate a massage along the outside of its teeth at first, but if you are patient and proceed with caution, in a week or so your pet should allow you to rub the tops and the insides of all its teeth.

Next substitute a soft-bristle, child's toothbrush (or a toothbrush designed especially for cats) for your finger and play "Brush the Kitty's Teeth." Smear a tiny dab of Nutri-Cal on the toothbrush—or dip the toothbrush in clam juice or the water from a tuna can—before you brush your cat's teeth.

As soon as your cat gets used to the idea of having its teeth brushed in this manner, switch to a malt-flavored feline toothpaste. (Feline toothpastes are available in sprays and solutions.)

Although your cat may not become wildly enamored of the idea, your pet should accept tooth brushing as part of its regular grooming routine. This will allow you to keep its teeth fairly clean and to stay aware of the condition of its teeth and gums, so that a dental problem will not go unnoticed for long if your cat does develop one.

Nursing a Sick Kitten

The way a kitten sees it, the best thing you can do for it when it is sick is to leave it alone. Young as they are, kittens appreciate the regenerative power of solitude, and they seek it out instinctively. They expect you to appreciate and to respect that power as well. Thus, to nurse a sick kitten is to strike a balance between respecting its desire for privacy and helping it to recover from what ails it.

Not surprisingly, kittens do not make the greatest patients. They resist taking pills as though they were being poisoned. They lick any "foreign" material from their coats, especially if it is medicated. They object to being force-fed, and because their instincts tell them they are vulnerable and, therefore, ought to hide when they are sick, they often must be caged so that you will be able to find them when it is time for a 2 a.m. medication.

For these reasons, if your kitten is seriously ill or injured, it is better left to the ministrations of your vet. Your kitten will miss you while it is in the hospital, and you will miss your kitten—in addition to feeling guilty for leaving the kitten at the vet's—but at least your kitten will not associate you with pills and other unpleasantries.

Lesser ailments and convalescence should be weathered at home in familiar surroundings. This means, of course, that pills and medications must be administered by familiar hands. Namely, yours.

The first principle of home nursing care is that sick or convalescing kittens should be isolated from other cats. The second rule is that persons handling sick or convalescing kittens should wash their hands thoroughly and change their clothes before handling other cats. In fact, anyone handling a sick kitten would do well to wear rubber gloves. What's more, all bedding, food dishes, water bowls, and litter pans used by any kitten suffering from a contagious disease should be disinfected with a nontoxic antiseptic. All leftover food, litter, soiled dressings, excrement, and other waste should be sealed in a plastic bag and placed immediately into an outdoor trash can.

Sick kittens are best confined to a double cage, 22 inches (56 cm) deep and tall and 44 inches (112 cm) wide in a warm, quiet, draft-free room. The cage should contain a litter pan, food dish, water bowl, and a cozy cat bed for the patient. You can make your kitten feel more secure by draping towels around three sides and over the top of the cage.

Though a sick kitten might not be up to playing with toys, hang a toy spider in one corner of the cage anyway. Your kitten may eventually find the spider diverting. If your kitten must be kept warm, put a cardboard box in one corner of the cage; put a heating pad covered with a towel in the bottom of the box, and cut down one side of the box to make it easy for your kitten to get in and out. Leave a radio, set to an easy-listening station, playing softly. Groom your kitten as usual if it will tolerate the attention. Otherwise, just hold your kitten and pet it gently—or merely sit there to keep the kitten company. Do not spend too much time with your kitten. Sleep is the second-best medicine in most cases.

Many sick kittens are not eager to eat, so you will be challenged to provide something that your kitten will find palatable. Do not worry over balanced diets for the moment. Feed a sick kitten anything it will eat. Remember that kittens recovering from upper respiratory infections may not be able to smell most foods. Therefore, use strong-smelling food like sardines or tuna fish or meat that has been seasoned liberally with garlic. If a kitten accepts any of these, be thankful. You can balance the menu as time passes and your kitten grows stronger.

A great favorite of sick kittens is sliced turkey breast from the deli. So is baby food. Some kittens will eat a molasses-like, high-calorie food substitute available from your veterinarian.

In order that your kitten does not become dehydrated, resort to any fluid you have to in order to get it to drink: chicken broth, water, beef broth, or evaporated milk mixed with baby cereal, egg yolk, karo syrup, and a pinch of salt. If your kitten is extremely weak, you may have to give it fluids with an eyedropper or a syringe.

Pilling a kitten is often a strenuous proposition at best. Some people seem to have been born with a knack for pilling. They grasp the top of a kitten's head in one hand, pinching the corners of its mouth with thumb and middle finger or ring finger to force the mouth open, drop the pill onto the back of the kitten's tongue, jab an index finger quickly against the back of its throat, withdraw the finger, hold the kitten's mouth shut, then blow quickly into the kitten's face to startle it and make it swallow.

Kitten owners lacking this agility and self-confidence resort to pill guns, which still require that someone pry open a kitten's mouth to insert the gun, or to hiding ground-up pills in butter, a lump of hamburger, or a mound of baby food. Whatever technique works, praise your pet for taking a pill and give it a treat afterward.

Force-feeding

Force-feeding is less strenuous on your kitten, and your pet's initial resistance may lessen when it realizes that the stuff you are putting into its mouth tastes good. The technique for force-feeding resembles that for pilling. Hold the kitten's head from the top. Place your thumb against one corner of the kitten's mouth and your middle or ring finger against the other corner. Squeeze until the kitten's mouth opens. Put a dollop of food on the index finger of your free hand and rub it onto the roof of your kitten's mouth. Relax the pressure on the sides of the kitten's face, allowing your kitten's mouth to close, but keep its head restrained or else the kitten might shake the food out all over you. Putting a small dab of food on the kitten's nose, from which it promptly will lick the morsel, is another way of getting your pet to take some nourishment.

If you are feeding liquid foods, put them into a syringe, open the kitten's mouth as above, then squeeze some of the liquid into the pocket formed where the kitten's upper and lower lips meet. Administer the liquid slowly, allowing the kitten time to swallow. Five-cc syringes are easily manipulated. Buy a supply of them and change them frequently.

Skin Medicating

Once you have applied any skin medication, hold your kitten or play with it quietly for a few minutes to distract it so that your pet will not lick the medication off at once before it has had a chance to do any good. If skin medication must remain undisturbed for a longer period of time, ask your vet to show you how to fashion an Elizabethan collar that will prevent the kitten from licking itself.

After the business of pilling, force feeding, or medicating your kitten is finished, apologize for the intrusion and explain that you are really trying to help. Then sit with your pet quietly for a while, commiserating.

Chapter 11

Understanding and Communicating with Your Kitten

It seems as though every other T-shirt, calendar, coffee mug, Christmas card, or notepad in the United States bears the image and likeness of a cat. Yet despite their present lionization, cats have not always been accorded such royal treatment. Cats have been deified and vilified, elevated and desecrated, revered and reviled. Indeed,

Kittens are good conversationalists because they listen more than they speak.

no other animal in history has been subject to such violent swings of fortune as the cat, and that fact has not been without consequence on the cat's development. The main truths in these consequences include a quiet independence, an inclination under most circumstances not involving food to greet any summons with indifference, a social distance that can make Attila the Hun look like Chuckles the Clown, and a tendency, through no fault of their own, to be grievously misunderstood for being so frequently misrepresented.

If the truth were known, however, cats are neither demon nor deity, and they certainly are not the haughty curmudgeons that some cartoonists and a few unenlightened feature writers make them out to be. Cats are not sly, paradoxical, arrogant, detached, ethereal, intimidating, or all that terribly intricate. Nor were they created so that humans might flatter themselves into thinking that when they pet a cat they are caressing the tiger. A cat is no one's stand-in.

Cats do possess a quiet sovereignty that some people find disquieting, and they are masters and mistresses at getting what they want while doing more or less what they wish. They are quite willing, nevertheless, to dance to our tunes occasionally, as long as we do not call a square dance when they are in the mood for a minuet. Cats are also quite willing to harmonize with us, as long as we do not sing off-key; and they are easily capable of poetry, although their tastes run more to a quiet lyric than to a full-blown epic. Indeed, cats are surprisingly adept at playing the clown, as long as they do not wind up with any holes in their dignity.

"So perhaps a small part of the cat's notorious reserve and aloofness is something like whistling in the dark," observed Lloyd Alexander, author of *My Five Tigers*, more than three decades ago, long before cats had become ubiquitous totems in our society. "A cat's life can be as difficult as our own. And it may be that we comfort them for being cats as much as they comfort us for being human."

The Effect of Domestication on Feline Behavior

The circumstances under which the cat was domesticated provide the chief clue to understanding the cat's behavior. According to zoologist F. E. Zeuner, humans had domesticated at least a dozen animals before establishing any sort of relationship with the cat. That relationship, which began roughly 3,600 years ago, was initiated as much by the cat as it was by anyone else.

The particulars regarding the who, where, and when of the cat's domestication are scanty, but the why is not so mysterious. Most researchers believe that cats were domesticated for rat and mice patrol and—to a lesser extent—for companionship. Wild cats, attracted by food refuse and by the large populations of mice and rats that thrived in human settlements, most likely

Sometimes we can hardly see the kitten for the forest.

moved closer to towns and villages over time. Controlling vermin was a grievous necessity in an agrarian society. Thus, as cats demonstrated their skill at protecting grain, farmers began feeding them to encourage them to stay on the job.

That was as formal as the arrangement got. No one has yet to provide any evidence that the cat's gradual acceptance into human lives was the result of any premeditation on the part of humans. Nor is there much evidence to refute the claim that the cat was and remains a self-domesticating animal.

If the circumstances of the cat's domestication differed from that of other animals, so did the cat's lifestyle. Other animals that humans have domesticated usually lived in some kind of communal arrangement. They also exhibited several

highly significant predictors of domestication: membership in a large social group, an acquaintance with a hierarchical group structure, omnivorous eating habits, adaptability to a wide range of environments, limited agility, the use of movements or posturing to advertise sexual receptivity, and a promiscuous lifestyle. The cat—bless its singular heart—lights up the scoreboard on only three of these traits: sexual posturing, promiscuity, and adaptability to a wide range of environments.

This helps to explain why the cat does not regard human beings with the same incessant affection as the dog or the same tote-that-barge stoicism as the horse. The horse, for example, follows the lead of the dominant member of the herd, usually the alpha mare. When that mare stops to graze, the herd chows down; when the mare skips off at a gallop, the herd follows.

This centuries-old, follow-the-leader instinct allows humans to assume the role of the alpha or dominant animal in the horse's life once the process of domestication occurs. In other words, it is not that difficult for humans to become top dog in Trigger's domain, but not in Garfield's, who was used to going his own way for thousands of centuries before signing a series of one-generation-only contracts to do light mouse work for humans. Thus, whereas the dog is prewired to seek the goodwill of the alpha human, the cat is inclined to offer its friendship to such as deserve it.

What's more, the interval since the cat was first domesticated is but a blink in time's steady gaze. During that interval cats have remained a compelling example of a species that is only in the first stage of domestication, capable of reverting to a feral state and not all that different from its ancestors. Described as the wildest of the tame animals and the tamest of wild ones, the domestic cat is, in one crucial sense, not truly domesticated at all. Humans have exercised little control over the cat's reproductive life—save for the occasional bucket of water tossed from a bedroom window in the middle of a howling night. If the conservative standard of domestication is applied to cats—a standard in which natural selection by the domesticated species has no

place—then the pedigreed cat is the only truly domesticated cat; and it has been domesticated for little more than one hundred years, the length of time that people have been keeping tabs on pedigrees.

This view of domestication helps to explain further the differences between cats' behavior and that of other domesticated animals, dogs especially. Unlike dogs—which were bred in the pursuit of a wide range of skills and temperament for centuries before they were bred for conformation alone—cats have virtually never been bred on purpose; and the ones that have, have been bred mainly for their physical traits.

Ultimately, such considerations are meaningless to the cat and its advocates. "The fact that cats associate with humans at all," says Alexander, "may indicate that they don't consider us such a bad lot."

Perhaps in time the cats will evolve into companions that are more fawning than formal. Cats are known for their ability to exploit the most precarious of niches. If people want cats to fetch the newspaper—and set about breeding cats selectively with that end in mind—the late twenty-first century feline no doubt will be described by writers as categorically different from the cat of the late-twentieth century. Who is to say, in fact, that the capacity for a more involved relationship with humans has not been part of the cat's repertoire all along? A talent the cat has been patiently waiting for us to discover.

Communal Living

Feral cats, wherever we find them—in the back alleys of our cities, the backyards of suburbia, and the back woods and country-side of rural America—lead solitary lives, much as their ancestors have done for millions of years. The chief characteristics of a cat's life are low population densities, well-estab-lished rituals, clearly defined territo-ries, limited and ritualized interac-tions between adult cats, and one-tom-per-neighborhood living arrangements.

Cats that live indoors, particularly in multicat arrangements, are pro-vided with regular meals and cli-mate-controlled lodging, but they are asked to tolerate conditions that violate the natural order. In one study of cat-population densities conducted in England, researchers found that feral cats in East London, where cats' living arrangements were the most crowded, had territo-ries that averaged two-hundredths of an acre or 871 square feet (81 square m). Small as that is by a cat's standards, it is a veritable kingdom compared with the amount of space in the typical households in which most cats live. Few house-holds are large enough to provide even this minimal acreage for every cat in residence. Obviously, indoor cats must live in smaller "territories" than do outdoor cats and, in multi-cat households, they must put up with greater interaction with other adult cats. These departures from a cat's natural lifestyle can lead to deviations in a cat's natural behav-ior and to greater susceptibility to stress and disease. The logistics of communal living may cause some cats to try to dominate others in the course of establishing a pecking order with regard to who eats before whom and to who sleeps in what window. Crowded living quar-ters may cause some cats to ignore their litter pans periodically and may result in the rapid spread of para-sites or illness if one member of the community becomes infected.

How Kittens Communicate

Vocal Communication

Communication includes the exchange of thoughts, feelings, needs, moods, information, trust, and desires. It involves listening as well as speaking, and where the kitten is concerned, it entails listening not only with our ears, but with our eyes, and speaking not only with our voices, but with our gestures, as well.

Kittens are not as good at expressing their emotions with their faces as are puppies. Kittens can move their whiskers and their ears in an impressive variety of ways, but they do not come equipped with the facial muscles necessary to produce the full range of expres-sions—from joy to indignation to a woebegone, hangdog self-pity—with which puppies manipulate their way into their owners' hearts. Thus, kittens rely more on vocal communication and on body language to reveal what is on their minds.

Some cat breeds, most notably the Siamese and its Oriental brethren, chatter unceasingly; but the domestic cat, for the most part, shows more respect for the sounds of silence. With the exception of females in season, domestic cats save their voices for special occasions: meowing dejectedly if they have been shut into a closet by accident, grousing sharply if you have snagged their fur while grooming them, or sounding the alarm when they want you to get up and fix breakfast. Kittens may also—for no apparent reason other than the spontaneous expression of their joy at being alive and in your company—pop into your lap with a jolly *chirrup*. (There are, of course, other vocalizations that kittens use when speaking to one another or to birds on the far side of a window.)

No matter what the occasion, when your kitten speaks to you, there is a reason. Unlike people, kittens seldom talk to admire the sound of their own voices. You should, therefore, respond when your kitten speaks. The kitten stuck in the closet wants to hear how sorry you are for its misfortune and how you will never let this indignity occur again. The kitten whose fur has been ruffled wants a similar apology. The kitten waking you up for breakfast would like a cheery "good morning" and some food on its plate. The kitten making a joyful noise would appreciate a soft "Hello," an attentive "What is it?" or a fond "You don't say?"

A kitten's most endearing verbal communication is the silent meow, which has to be seen to be appreciated. A silent meow occurs when a cat opens its mouth and mimes the word *meow* but no sound emerges. Silent meows function as greetings, terms of endearment, all-purpose, unspecified complaints, and as the feline equivalents of baying at the moon.

"What do you mean you never promised me a rose garden?"

Body Language

Kittens are more likely to communicate with their bodies than with their voices. From the tips of their noses to the ends of their tails, kittens are like electronic bulletin boards on which a continuous series of messages flows.

Kittens generate at least three of those messages with their tails. Carried erect at a 90°angle to the body, the tail broadcasts a message of good cheer and camaraderie. Carried at a less jaunty angle and puffed out in bristling display, the tail is a declaration of war. Twitching slowly from side to side, the tail signals annoyance. The faster the twitch, the greater the itch; and if twitch turns to lash, beware. Fireworks are about to ensue.

At the other end of the message board, wide open, attentive eyes signal interest, in a positive fashion, in what a kitten sees; whereas a narrow gaze indicates that the kitten is not sure if what it sees is interesting or threatening. Kittens that gaze at a person and then blink their eyes slowly are sending a message of submission, much as one kitten will blink at another by way of de-escalating a face-to-face encounter.

A kitten uses its hindquarters to declare affection and trust. This form of communication—in which a kitten brushes past the object of its affection and then positions its hindquarters in firsthand proximity to the object's face—may take the kitten-owning novice by surprise, especially if kitten and novice are enjoying a nap together. Indeed, most longtime cat owners would prefer that their cats said it with flowers or a fax instead.

The full-body flop—a maneuver in which a kitten lands first on its side, then rolls onto its back, finally ending up in a semicircle—is a more conventional expression of fondness. This fetching invitation to a belly rub is usually inspired by a kitten's exuberance at being stroked along its spine or scratched at the base of its tail. Be cautious in accepting this invitation, however, because many kittens are ticklish on their bellies. When you reach

This inquisitive kitten's tail almost forms a question mark.

past their upturned paws to scratch their bellies, you are putting your arm at some risk. Should the kitten take a notion to grasp your arm between its front paws and to rabbit kick your arm with its back paws, you could be in for a bloodletting. Do not panic and try to withdraw your arm suddenly. That will make your situation more perilous because you will be pulling your tender skin against your kitten's talonlike claws. Instead of moving your arm backward toward you, move it forward and down through the kitten's front legs. Because that is the direction in which your upside-down kitten's claws are pointed, you will be disengaging your flesh from their grasp.

Right side up, the kitten taps out a variety of messages with its paws. A paw raised softly to a person's cheek or laid gently on the arm is a sign of attachment. A series of taps on the leg or arm is an attempt to bring a person to attention. A smart *whap* with the claws sheathed is a warning that you have violated a kitten's sense of propriety. Such warnings often are issued while a kitten is being groomed, usually in a spot that is sensitive or ticklish.

A kitten's ears, like its tail, convey different messages and emotions. Kittens swivel their ears in response to new sounds in the vicinity. They flatten their ears and extend them to the side in response to a frightening stimulus, and they will curl their ears backward in anger.

Socks Gilbeau, all-star goalie for the Birman Bibliopoles soccer team.

Kittens greet their friends—two-legged and four-legged alike—in well-scripted ceremonies. A kitten, its tail erect in greeting, will approach a friend and then rub its cheek against the cheek, neck, or face of that friend. This rite not only indicates cordiality, it is a request for permission to enter another individual's air space, and it leaves a trace of the approaching kitten's scent on its friend.

A kitten's facial muscles may lack the mobility needed to produce a broad range of expressions, but its body is an open book that reveals much about what a kitten is thinking and feeling. Arched backs and big tails, for example, are obvious signs of fear and displeasure. A low-slung advance with eyes and tail at half mast is a sign of attack, and a kitten

121

that has been reprimanded will sit frequently with its back to its owner to signal its indignation.

Communicating with Your Kitten

Kittens are more comfortable when humans communicate with them on their level than when approached from a superior position—looming large is often associated with predators. Therefore, when you are greeting a kitten, crouch down before you do and extend your slightly curled hand, knuckles facing away from you, toward the kitten, allowing it a chance to sniff your hand if the kitten wishes. If the kitten turns away from your hand, do not attempt to pet it right then because its behavior indicates a lack of interest in either you or your salutation.

When you interact with a kitten, try to mimic its sense of order, civility, and decorum. Do not make any abrupt movements or any sudden, loud noises. Do not lift the kitten up if it does not enjoy being carried, and by all means do not stare long and lovingly into its eyes. Kittens regard staring as an insult.

The Bond Between Humans and Cats

Despite their reputation for being aloof, cats are inclined to treat vir-tually every strange vertebrate they meet as a fellow cat—as long as that vertebrate does not trigger a cat's hunting instincts by making the rustling, squeaking, or scratching sounds that spell p-r-e-y to a cat. Therefore, absent any unpleasant experiences with humankind, cats are wont to regard the people they meet as fellow cats, too. Indeed, wrote German zoologist Paul Leyhausen in Cat Behavior, cats generally form closer bonds with humans than with other cats.

Leyhausen, who kept scores of cats for systematic, day-to-day observation, believed that cats housed together in large numbers, either for research or for breeding purposes, could not satisfy their social needs by contact with one another. He also believed that cats living as house pets needed human contact, too.

Leyhausen puzzled over the fact that cats that shunned or fought with other cats in the wild still retained the capacity for close relationships with humans. He theorized that juvenile habits in mammals do not disappear altogether. They are merely suppressed by other, adult activities and may occasionally reappear in the adult animal.

The adult activities that suppress the expression of juvenile habits include guarding territory, rearing young, fighting with rival cats, and seeking opportunities to mate. These activities, said Leyhausen, are so powerful in the adult cat that the inclination to juvenile activities

is seldom expressed once a cat reaches maturity. This inclination, however infrequently it finds expression, might nevertheless be the catalyst for what little sociability there is among adult felines, Leyhausen concluded.

For their part, people are simpatico enough in the eyes of a cat to merit a social relationship. Cat owners who understand this tendency and who take the time to cultivate it, said Leyhausen, may be able to inspire and even rejuvenate a cat's inclination for kittenish behavior. Humans do not raise a cat's hackles the way another cat will do; and humans are, as a result, privileged to enjoy the sort of genuine, lasting friendship that seldom occurs between two solitary, free-roaming cats.

Chapter 12
Contracts

In *Everybody's Guide to the Law* (Harper & Row, 1986), Melvin Belli and Allen P. Wilkinson write, "Of all the areas of law, none is encountered more frequently in day-to-day living than the law of contracts." Indeed, a day without contracts is a day without commercial interaction. People make contracts when they buy groceries at the supermarket, food in a restaurant, or tickets at a theater. A checking account is the subject of a contract with a bank; the newspaper waiting on the front porch or thereabouts is evidence of a contract with a publisher; and magazines are delivered pursuant to a contract with their publishers.

For all their ubiquity, the nice thing about contracts is, you do not need a lawyer—or even a notary—to make one. Any cat breeder of sound mind, sober mien, and sufficient age (generally 18) who is not an enemy alien or a convict doing hard time can make a contract with any other person of similar standing. Yet even though you can get by without a lawyer, you cannot get around the obligation of playing by the rules of law when you enter into a contract; for all contracts are subject to review in court, and the court can be a fussy proofreader.

The Origin of Contracts

According to E. Allan Farnsworth, professor of law at Columbia University, "the notion that a promise itself may give rise to an enforceable duty was an achievement of Roman law." (Little Brown & Company, 1982). But with the decline and fall of Rome went the Roman legal system. Bit by bit English courts had to redefine contract law during the Middle Ages."

The Parts of a Contract

The fruits of those labors, the laws governing contracts today, stipulate that a contract consists of an offer, an acceptance, and a consideration between parties who have the legal capacity to make a contract. In most states, persons who are sane, sober, and old enough can enter into contracts.

Persons who are incompetent, too drunk, or too stoned to understand the effects of a contract cannot. More precisely, they can make a contract, but they are not necessarily bound by its provisions.

A valid contract begins with an offer to establish an agreement between two parties. In addition to being indisputably clear, an offer must contain the names of the parties to the proposed contract, the subject matter of the contract, the price, and the time limit in which the contract must be performed.

One thing an offer does not have to contain is writing. Despite the wisdom of moviemaker Samuel Goldwyn's observation, "a verbal contract isn't worth the paper it's written on," Melvin Belli points out that an oral contract is as legally binding as a written one. But it is not just as easy to enforce if the parties disagree about what they agreed on. In order to protect your interests as well as your friendships, be sure that any contract you make is conveyed in writing.

Because an offer, according to the second part of Farnsworth's definition, is "conditional on a manifestation of assent" by the person to whom the offer was made (the offeree), a contract must also contain an acceptance: an it's-a-deal response from the offeree. This response can be verbal, written, or a profound inclination of the head.

At the heart of every contract is the consideration: something either given or promised in exchange for a promise. In breeders' contracts the something either given or promised is a cat, kitten, or stud service, and the promise given in exchange is usually the promise to send money or a *kittenback*. (A kittenback is a variable-worth form of currency, as evidenced by the abundant forms of the expression, "I'll let you have this kitten for $___.__ or a kittenback.")

Murphy's Law

These are the ties that bind offerer and offeree in a contract; but there is another law that persons buying a kitten must consider: the law promulgated by that esteemed legal scholar Murphy, who opined that if anything can possibly go wrong, it will. Therefore, we need to cross-examine the elements of a contract with an eye toward the possibilities for misfortune that lurk within each.

There is not too much that can go wrong in the neighborhood of legal capacity. A kitten buyer can generally tell (or inquire) if a person selling a kitten is daft, drunk, or underage. Moreover, most kitten contracts are made between principals, not agents, so there is seldom any need to mess with Mr. or Ms. In-between. If you should be approached by somebody's agent, always ask to see a copy of the agent's authority in writing, and ask the agent to state, again in writing, whether or not the person he or she represents has put any price limitations or other conditions on the terms of the sale.

Once we paddle out from the shore of contractual authority into the tides of offers, acceptances, and revocations, the legal waters become deeper and more troublesome. Suppose, for example, you are at a show and a breeder says, "If somebody offered me $15 for this lousy cat, I'd take it." Should you whip out your checkbook? No, because offers made in jest are not binding.

Slips of the Pen

Offers that contain mistakes are binding, however. If the owner of an orchard offers to sell 250 bushels of apples at $15 each when he meant to say 215, the owner of a fruit stand who accepts the offer without having any knowledge of the seller's mistake can recover for loss of expectation if the seller fails to deliver 250 bushels. So if a person selling a kitten means to set the price of the kitten at $750, he or she had better not type $700 on the contract instead.

Revoking an Offer

Although an offer "confers on the offeree the power to create a contract," the offerer has the power to revoke an offer before it is accepted. If, for instance, a person offers to sell you a kitten for $500, and he or she gives you a week to think it over, that person can revoke the offer at any time before you make your reply.

Keep in mind, however, that unlike an acceptance, which is effective upon dispatch—i.e., as soon as the offeree drops a correctly addressed letter bearing the proper amount of postage into a mailbox—a revocation becomes effective only upon receipt. Thus, if the breeder who offered you a kitten writes you a note to say that he or she has had a change of heart, but the note does not arrive until the day after you have mailed the seller a letter saying that you want the kitten, the seller's offer still stands. It would also stand if the seller had called you to revoke the offer but was not able to reach you before your acceptance arrived in the mail. And the offer would certainly stand if the seller had accepted money or some other consideration in return for keeping the offer open. In this case you and the seller have an "option contract," and the seller cannot revoke the offer.

On the other hand, if you reject an offer then turn around and inform the seller a few hours later that you want to accept that offer, the seller is not bound to accept your acceptance. An offer dies the moment it is rejected.

Finally, your acceptance of the offer must be unconditional and unequivocal. If you say, "I'll take the kitten if you let me bring her back for stud service," and the seller says, "No," then the deal is off. A conditional acceptance—which is what you made when you asked the seller to throw in stud service—has the same legal effect as a counteroffer: It terminates the original offer.

(Incidentally, the only person who can accept an offer is the person to whom the offer was made or that person's duly authorized agent. If someone offers to sell you a kitten and your friend Jane overhears this and says, "I'll buy it if she doesn't," the seller is not bound to sell the cat to Jane at the same price—or at all.)

The Consideration

The consideration—the raison d'etre of every contract—is perhaps its least troublesome area, especially in kitten contracts, where the seller's consideration is a kitten, cat, or stud service and the buyer's consideration is money or a kitten-back. The key to understanding considerations is remembering that they are two-way streets. If only one party makes a consideration, that's a gift; and gifts, like offers made in jest, are not binding.

Strings Attached to Contracts

There is a corollary of Murphy's Law of Contracts that dictates that the possibility of litigation is directly proportional to the number of strings attached to a contract, and breeders' contracts, unfortunately, often come equipped with more strings than the Boston Pops Orchestra. Some of those strings, however, are out of tune in a legal composition.

Many contracts specify that a kitten offered for sale cannot be declawed. But a breeder could run into problems trying to enforce that contract. What if the cat is destroying furniture in its new home and the owners have tried every possible method of getting it to stop? Or what if the sellers live a thousand miles away from the cat's owners? How are the former going to know if the latter are abiding by a questionable clause in a contract?

Sellers might also run into trouble if their contracts specify that a kitten offered for sale must not be allowed to go outside. Another source of difficulty is the buy-back clause, in which the seller specifies that he or she must be given first option of buying a cat back at the original price if the buyer decides to sell or place it. The part about the right of first refusal is fine, but the original price part is not. The seller would be better off saying, "at the going rate for cats of this breed when the buyer decides to sell it." By insisting on buying a cat back at the original price, the seller is depriving the buyer of the right to benefit from the time and money he or she puts into the cat and from any increase in the cat's value because of its breeding or showring achievements.

The going rate for the cat is often determined by what someone else is willing to pay for it. If you buy a kitten for $750 and two years later you have a legitimate offer of $1,000 from someone who wants to buy the kitten, the latter is the going rate.

Breeders lard their contracts with hordes of provisions in hopes of protecting their kittens as much as possible. Such intentions are laudable, but they are not always legal, especially when they are tantamount to taking the law into their own hands. Thus, breeders should not include in a contract the amount of penalty a buyer will

"Are you blind, ump? That ball was clearly out."

have to pay for violating any part of that contract. (They can include it of course, but that does not mean a court is going to take them seriously.) Nor should a breeder specify that any trial that arises as a result of the buyer breaching the contract will occur in the breeder's home state, and the buyer will be responsible for court costs and attorneys' fees. These are matters for a court to decide. What's more, in interstate cases a federal court automatically has jurisdiction. The federal court may decide to change the venue to another state, but a breeder cannot make that determination.

Breeders' Rights

Despite the need for caution and realistic expectations in drawing up a contract, a breeder is not without certain rights. Breeders can enforce contracts that specify that the buyer of a kitten cannot sell the kitten—or any of its future off-spring—to a pet shop, animal dealer, or research lab. (There would not be any justice in the world if a breeder could not do that.) But it would not be a good idea for a breeder to name individual persons with whom the buyer cannot do business. A breeder can also expect to be able to enforce a stipulation that says that a kitten cannot be used for breeding or showing—though it would not be wise to specify that a cat can only be shown in a certain association.

Modifying a Contract

Contracts once signed, though binding, are not carved in stone. They can be modified in writing or verbally, even if they contain a clause stating that they cannot be modified verbally. But if a contract is to be modified, there must be an additional consideration. For example, if a breeder offers to sell a cat for $1,000 and the offeree accepts and a month later the breeder calls to say that the cat has improved and the price is now $1,250, the offeree is not bound to accept the new-and-improved price, but the seller is still bound to honor the contract. And even if the buyer says OK to the new price, he or she is not bound by that acceptance because the seller did not offer any additional consideration that justified the additional money.

Because contract law varies from one state to another, you should consult an attorney before entering into a contract if you have any questions about its provisions. And if you should get into a dispute over a contract, do not take the law into your own hands, you take them to court.

Useful Literature and Addresses

Books

Behrend, K. and Wegler, M. *The Complete Book of Cat Care: How to Raise a Happy and Healthy Cat.* Barron's Educational Series, Inc., Hauppauge, New York, 1991.

Carlson, Delbert G., D.V.M., and Giffin, James M., M.D. *Cat Owner's Veterinary Handbook,* New York: Howell Book House, 1983.

Daly, Carol Himsel, D.V.M. *Caring for Your Sick Cat.* Barron's Educational Series, Inc., Hauppauge, New York, 1994.

Fogle, Bruce. *The Cat's Mind: Understanding Your Cat's Behavior.* New York: Howell Book House, 1992.

Frye, Fredric. *First Aid for Your Cat.* Barron's Educational Series, Inc., Hauppauge, New York, 1987.

Maggitti, Phil. *Guide to a Well-Behaved Cat.* Barron's Educational Series, Inc., Hauppauge, New York, 1993.

Tabor, Roger. *The Wild Life of the Domestic Cat.* London: Arrow Books Limited, 1983.

Turner, Dennis C. and Bateson, Patrick, eds. *The Domestic Cat: the Biology of its Behavior.* Cambridge, England: Cambridge University Press, 1988.

Wright, Michael and Walters, Sally, ed. *The Book of the Cat.* New York, Summit Books, 1980.

Cat Registries

American Cat Association
8101 Katherine Avenue
Panorama City, CA 91402
818-782-6080

American Cat Fanciers Association
P.O. Box 203
Point Lookout, MO 65726
417-334-5430

Canadian Cat Association
83 Kennedy Road South
Unit 1805
Brampton, Ontario
Canada L6W 3P3
905-459-1481

Cat Fanciers' Association
P.O. Box 1005
Manasquan, NJ 08738-1005
908-528-9797

Cat Fanciers' Federation
9509 Montgomery Road
Cincinnati, OH 45242
513-984-1841

The International Cat Association
P.O. Box 2684
Harlingen, TX 78551
210-428-8046

Cat Magazines

Cats
2750-A South Ridgewood Avenue
South Daytona, FL 32119

Cat Fancy
P.O. Box 6050
Mission Viejo, CA 92690

Index